T0211457

# Computer
# Supported
# Cooperative Work

# *Advanced Topics in Organizational Behavior*

The **Advanced Topics in Organizational Behavior** series examines current and emerging issues in the field of organizational behavior. Written by researchers who are widely acknowledged subject area experts, the books provide an authoritative, up-to-date review of the conceptual, research, and practical implications of the major issues in organizational behavior.

# Computer Supported Cooperative Work

## Issues and Implications for Workers, Organizations, and Human Resource Management

Michael D. Coovert
Lori Foster Thompson

Advanced Topics in
Organizational Behavior

**Sage Publications**
*International Educational and Professional Publisher*
Thousand Oaks ■ London ■ New Delhi

*For information:*

 Sage Publications, Inc.
2455 Teller Road
Thousand Oaks, California 91320
E-mail: order@sagepub.com

Sage Publications Ltd.
6 Bonhill Street
London EC2A 4PU
United Kingdom

Sage Publications India Pvt. Ltd.
M-32 Market
Greater Kailash I
New Delhi 110 048 India


*Library of Congress Cataloging-in-Publication Data*

Coovert, Michael D.
Computer supported cooperative work: Issues and implications for workers, organizations, and human resource management / by Michael D. Coovert, Lori Foster Thompson
    p. cm. — (Advanced topics in organizational behavior)
    ISBN 0-7619-0572-3 (cloth: alk. paper)
    ISBN 0-7619-0573-1 (pbk.: alk. paper)
1.  Teams in the workplace—Data prcessing.  2. Employees—Effect of technological innovations on.  3. Groupware (Computer software)  4. Microcomputer workstations.  5. Industrial sociology.  6. Organizational behavior. I. Thompson, Lori L. II. Title. III. Series
HD66.2 .C665 2000
658.4'036'0285416—dc21

                                                                                    00-011773


01   02   03   04   05   06   10   9   8   7   6   5   4   3   2   1

| | |
|---|---|
| *Acquiring Editor:* | Marquita Flemming |
| *Editorial Assistant:* | MaryAnn Vail |
| *Production Editor:* | Nevair Kabakian |
| *Editorial Assistant:* | Victoria Cheng |
| *Typesetter:* | Denyse Dunn |
| *Indexer:* | Michael Ferreira |

# *Contents*

*To Mae, who with the help of David Coovert, skillfully raised nine children with no computer support.*

*and*

*To Sharon and Fred Foster, who expertly taught their seven kids the value of cooperative work.*

# *Preface*

The world in which we live continues to be rapidly affected by technology. Perhaps nowhere are these changes being felt more dramatically than in the workplace. The latest innovations invariably create new opportunities, challenges, and concerns for the workers who are required to use them. Many of these issues involve employees' interactions with new technology as well as the extent to which technology facilitates collaboration among coworkers. Computer supported cooperative work (CSCW) is a field that explores these and related topics, which emerge when individuals use technology in the workplace.

The purpose of this book is to provide an introduction to CSCW and to discuss its implications for organizations, managers, and employees performing various types of collaborative work. We focus on general trends in computer support, the characteristics and technological requirements of workers engaged in different levels of cooperation, the current and future directions of CSCW, and the implications of CSCW for human resource management. In the discussion of these implications, we address a number of important organizational topics, providing our perspective on the likely ramifications of CSCW for managers and for those working with organizational personnel. We do not, however, present an exhaustive treatment of human resource management. Such an approach, which could fill multiple volumes, is beyond the scope of this book.

Our discussion of CSCW includes a number of exciting innovations designed to aid collaborative work. We address these CSCW technologies at a conceptual level to provide the reader with a feel for their application in the work world. We do not offer specific detail on the *technical* aspects of CSCW hardware and software. Furthermore, we do not provide a comprehensive list of all currently available collaborative technologies. Rather, we highlight various innovations to illustrate CSCW in action.

This book is appropriate for anyone interested in the topic of CSCW. In other words, the reader does not need to be a computer specialist to understand this treatment of the subject matter. We anticipate that the book will be especially useful for business practitioners whose workplaces include CSCW and for those who are considering the implementation of CSCW technologies. This book should also prove useful in the classroom as a text for CSCW courses or as a supplement to the materials required for certain advanced business, psychology, and computer science courses. Software developers and other specialists who create CSCW tools may benefit from this reading, as will researchers interested in empirically investigating CSCW and its impact within a variety of disciplines.

The material in this book is divided into six chapters. The first chapter provides a general overview of CSCW and argues that the field is best understood by delineating the terms *computer support* and *cooperative work*. Chapter 2 addresses the *computer-supported* side of the equation by presenting several current and emerging trends in CSCW systems. These trends involve new tools (e.g., intelligent agents), and they also include recent and upcoming strategies for interacting with technology (e.g., nomadic computing). Specific CSCW technologies are highlighted in Chapter 2 to illustrate different trends in contemporary computing. Chapter 3 focuses on *cooperative work* by describing and distinguishing different levels of collaboration, such as individual work, group work, and teamwork. Chapter 3 is based on the premise that technology will facilitate collaborative work most effectively when it supports the level or type of cooperation required by the task at hand. Chapter 4 discusses the current and future directions of CSCW, from both a behavioral and a technical standpoint. From a behavioral point of view, this chapter highlights some current research findings and considers how behavioral CSCW research questions might be approached in the future. From a technical perspective, Chapter 4 addresses current and future CSCW philosophies, offering a peek into the exciting future of *cooperative buildings,* which can be constructed to enable multiple levels of collaboration simultaneously. Because emerging CSCW technologies will undoubtedly affect the people who work through and with them, Chapter 5 addresses the implications of CSCW for human resource management (HRM). Chapter 5 discusses the changing job and worker requirements that accompany CSCW, speculating on the likely implications for various aspects of HRM, such as selection, training, leadership, and performance appraisal. Finally, Chapter 6 offers concluding remarks regarding CSCW and its role in organizations.

Where appropriate, we direct the interested reader to Web sites corresponding to various topics discussed in these chapters. Moreover, this book itself has a Web page, which can be accessed from both authors' home pages:

- luna.cas.usf.edu/~coovert/
- core.ecu.edu/psyc/fosterl/foster.html

From the sites listed above, access the book's Web page for direct links to the sites described in this text. Because many Internet addresses are time sensitive, we will use this book's Web page to update our in-text links as they change.

Before advancing to the first chapter, we would like to thank our colleagues, friends, and families, who assisted us in countless ways during the completion of this book. We are especially grateful for the support provided by Paul Spector, Kevin Kelloway, David and Molly Coovert, and Windsor Thompson.

# 1

# *Overview of CSCW*

**Chapter Outline**

The Origins and Development of Computer Supported Cooperative
Work (CSCW)

The Topics and Community Driving CSCW

Summary: CSCW's Definitional Quandary

**Key Concepts**

1. **Asynchronous Communication.** Communication that does not occur
   simultaneously (e.g., standard e-mail conversations).
2. **Computer Supported Cooperative Work (CSCW).** Comprises a
   field of study that addresses the implications of technology in collaborative work settings. Combines the investigation of cooperative work
   with the enabling technologies of computer networking and associated
   hardware, software, services, and techniques.
3. **Local Area Network (LAN).** A network of interconnected, personal
   computers that are able to share resources and communicate directly
   with other devices in the network.
4. **Personal Computer (PC).** A general-purpose computer equipped with
   a microprocessor and designed to run commercial software for an individual user. Usually refers to machines that conform to the standard of
   the IBM PC.
5. **Real-time Communication.** Concurrent conversations that take place,
   for example, between two face-to-face individuals.

Almost every work organization depends on technology. Technology can serve a variety of purposes, including the facilitation of employee collaboration. For example, Nissan executives throughout the world use handheld computers to retrieve e-mail, communicate with one another, and gain remote access to their company's computer network (Gomes & Bransten, 1997). Workers in other organizations, such as AT&T, Bell Atlantic, and the Carrier Corporation hold routine video conferences, which may include interviewing, brainstorming, troubleshooting, and long-distance training sessions (Gale, 1994; Keates, 1997; Ziegler, 1994). Whether they know it or not, employees such as these are engaged in computer supported cooperative work (CSCW)—an activity that has generated a considerable amount of interest during the past two decades.

CSCW is a field of study that addresses the implications of technology in collaborative work settings. It combines the investigation of cooperative work (i.e., any work involving collaboration among humans) with the enabling technologies of computer networking and associated hardware, software, services, and techniques (Wilson, 1991). The overall objective of CSCW involves a greater understanding of the requirements for, the development of, and the effects of innovative technologies during cooperative work (Greenberg & Neuwirth, 1998). In other words, it is concerned with how technology can help people work together more effectively.

Interest in CSCW is spreading rapidly because developments in this area benefit several distinct segments of the population. The field of CSCW helps workers by promoting the conception and implementation of powerful technologies that allow employees to collaborate naturally while enhancing their individual, group, and team skills (Coovert, 1995). For example, under the right circumstances, video conferencing technologies can facilitate effective long-distance collaboration better than can a traditional telephone. CSCW benefits organizations by improving employees' productivity and increasing businesses' profitability (Wilson, 1994). Consider the travel money that an organization saves when CSCW technologies allow employees who are geographically separated from one another to collaborate without traveling. Finally, CSCW research and conferences serve computer scientists by providing insights into the technological requirements of human beings and by putting software developers and various other specialists in touch with their business markets.

## The Origins and Development of CSCW

CSCW is a relatively new topic of interest, and its recent emergence can be attributed to at least three developments in technology and the modern work organization. First, CSCW arose largely because of the development of the microprocessor and the desktop personal computer (PC), which were introduced by IBM in 1981. The original $2,800 price of this stand-alone desktop machine sharply contrasted with the million-dollar mainframe computer of the 1960s. Following its introduction, this smaller, faster, cheaper machine quickly became the industry standard, promoting the use of computers at work by providing new information technology to a large, nontechnical segment of the organization. For the first time, computing power was placed in the hands of employees who were not computer specialists (Craiger, 1997; Scrivener, 1994; Tapscott & Caston, 1993; Van der Spiegel, 1995).

A second technological advance closely followed the arrival of the PC and further contributed to the development of CSCW. Organizations began to recognize the need to connect desktop PCs, thereby allowing computers and their operators to exchange data and communicate with one another. New local area network (LAN) and client server network technology emerged and began to enable such connectivity in the 1980s, facilitating collaboration among employees. In short, the personal computer became the interpersonal computer (Craiger, 1997; Johansen, 1988; Scrivener, 1994).

The increasing use of teams in organizations is the third factor that drove the initiation of CSCW as a formal area of inquiry. Rapid changes in the economic climate, broad organizational access to information technology, and the globalization of the marketplace prompted the trend toward teamwork in the 1980s and beyond (Spurr, Layzell, Jennison, & Richards, 1994; Tapscott & Caston, 1993). Due to the preceding technological advancements, these increasingly common teamwork activities often involved computers.

Irene Greif and Paul Cashman coined the phrase *computer supported cooperative work* and used it as the title of a workshop in 1984. The workshop was designed to address concerns about clusters of individuals working together with computer systems (Bannon & Schmidt, 1991). The issues ranged from the suitability of different types of media (text, image, video, and voice) to the understanding of team processes (Wilson, 1991). The positive, interdisciplinary response to the first CSCW workshop furthered development of the field.

CSCW's current acceptance is demonstrated by the fact that various countries now host yearly CSCW conferences, and a number of college courses, Web sites, articles, and electronic news sources have been dedicated to the subject matter. (At the time of this writing, www.UsabilityFirst.com/cscw.html provides an excellent index of CSCW resources, including a listing of conferences and workshops, journals, products and companies, special interest groups, and newsgroups.)

## *The Topics and Community Driving CSCW*

Topics of interest in the field of CSCW include all of the mainstream aspects of group and team research, as well as areas related to technological development (Coovert, 1995). (Group work and teamwork will be discussed further in Chapter 2.) Table 1.1, which lists the topics covered during a recent CSCW conference, demonstrates several different emphases within the field. As Table 1.1 reveals, some CSCW issues are fundamentally behavioral (e.g., the investigation of the relationships between team members' perceptions of communication overload and their overall performance). In contrast, other topics are primarily technical (e.g., the development of mobile computing, telemanipulation, and wearable computer technologies). It is important to note that although current writings often emphasize either human behavior or technology, CSCW does not typically address one component at the utter exclusion of the other. Indeed, it is the relationship between the behavioral and technical elements that makes CSCW unique and valuable (Wilson, 1994).

Within this technological and behavioral framework, CSCW research addresses a wide variety of issues. It embraces the exploration of every type of collaborative technology imaginable. Furthermore, it involves the investigation of these collaborative technologies in the context of the single worker, pairs of employees, small clusters, large groups, and entire organizations. CSCW addresses both face-to-face and dispersed teamwork, and it examines both real-time and asynchronous cooperation (Scrivener & Clark, 1994; Wilson, 1994). *Real-time* refers to concurrent conversations that take place, for example, between two face-to-face individuals. *Asynchronous* refers to communication that does not occur at the same time, such as standard e-mail conversations.

Undoubtedly, this type of variety draws an interesting and diverse community of scientists, scholars, and practitioners. CSCW is a truly interdisciplinary

**TABLE 1.1** Issues Addressed During a Recent CSCW Conference

| *General Category* | *Example Topic(s) Within Each General Category* |
| --- | --- |
| Studies of work that result in the identification of new research problems and design requirements for CSCW architectures and applications. | Research regarding the identification of potential collaborative partners. |
| The development of new technologies and the identification of requirements for their use in collaborative work. | Research and development efforts surrounding mobile computing, tele-manipulation, and wearable computer technology. |
| The development of innovative prototypes and techniques designed to solve or mitigate problems that users experience with current systems. | The mitigation of users' sense of intrusiveness in video systems. |
| The investigation of architectures to support group activity more effectively. | The development of scalable, reliable protocols across heterogeneous platforms. Rapid, end-user construction of collaborative applications and run-time change of coordination policies |
| The clarification of key theoretical concepts. | Discussions of *awareness* and *organizational memory*. |
| The development of better frameworks and empirical measures that predict collaborative success. | The investigation of the relationships between team members' perceptions of communication overload and their overall performance. |
| The development of new models of the social and organizational effects of technology. | The exploration of factors influencing computer-mediated conversations among hundreds of people. |

SOURCE: Adapted from Greenberg and Neuwirth (1998). Used by permission.

field, with participation from specialists in anthropology, business, cognition, computer science (especially those concerned with networks, messaging services, and distributed systems), ergonomics, human-computer interaction, human factors, information technology, office automation, organizational design, psychology, and sociology. In addition, CSCW has attracted the interest of consultants, managers, vendors of collaborative technologies, workers, and general users (Bowers & Benford, 1991; Scrivener & Clark, 1994; Spurr et al., 1994; Wilson, 1991).

## Summary: CSCW's Definitional Quandary

The emergence and general nature of CSCW are relatively clear. Nevertheless, the broad interdisciplinary scope and rapid development of CSCW make it difficult to assign a precise definition to the field. Indeed, Bannon and Schmidt (1991) contend that the unique, identifying elements are disturbingly obscure, referring to CSCW as "four characters in search of a context." Today, practitioners and scholars continue to debate the exact meaning of the acronym. Although some equate CSCW with computer aids and enabling technologies, opponents assert that a technology-driven approach may serve to confuse and undermine both research and practice within the field of CSCW. This latter argument is consistent with the notion that CSCW is best conceived of as an endeavor to understand the characteristics of cooperative work behavior with the objective of designing adequate technology to support it (Bannon & Schmidt, 1991).

Because it has been suggested that CSCW cannot be properly understood until each of its components, *CS* and *CW,* are delineated, the next two chapters unwrap the acronym by discussing key issues involved in computer support and cooperative work, respectively.

# 2

# *Computer Support*

**Chapter Outline**

**Key Concepts**

1. **Artificial Intelligence (AI).** An area of science that focuses on a machine's ability to simulate human intelligence processes.
2. **Augmented Reality.** A virtual world that is presented within the real world, thus enhancing, as opposed to replacing, the physical world. Accomplished by creating the illusion of transparency and by generating rays of light to form computer-generated *overlays*.
3. **Chording Keyboard.** Keyboard that allows a user to input a word by pressing a series of keys simultaneously.

4. **Computer Aided Design (CAD).** The use of computer graphics to create precision drawings or technical illustrations that would have been accomplished with pencil and paper in days gone by. CAD software is used by drafters, architects, engineers, and others. Can be used to create both 2-dimensional (2D) drawings and 3-dimensional (3D) models.

5. **Computer Support.** A constantly changing term. Refers to goal-enabling technologies and their associated hardware, software, services, and techniques.

6. **Direct Manipulation Technology.** Technology that requires users to explicitly initiate all tasks and monitor all events.

7. **Expert System.** Computer system that uses a database (or knowledge base) containing the knowledge and problem-solving heuristics of experts as well as control strategies that allow the computer to arrive at the same conclusions that an expert would.

8. **Extended Reality.** Replacing or enhancing the physical environment with electronic images and objects, as with virtual and augmented reality respectively.

9. **Graphical User Interface (GUI).** An interface that typically allows users to interact with computers by making choices via windows, menus, icons, and various point devices.

10. **Haptic.** Having to do with the sense of touch. From the Greek word *haptein.*

11. **Heads-Up Display.** An electronically generated output of information superimposed on a user's forward field of view.

12. **Inferential Capability.** The ability to go beyond concrete instructions and use symbolic abstraction to solve problems.

13. **Intelligent Agent Technology.** A computer program that performs tasks without direct human supervision. An intelligent agent is considered to be an assistant or helper rather than a conventional electronic tool.

14. **Knowledge Engineering.** The process of extracting expert knowledge and encoding it for computer use.

15. **Multimodal Interface.** An interface that accepts many types of input from a user (e.g., combinations of speech, pen, and gesture), while providing multimedia output (e.g., combinations of video, audio, and tactile feedback).

16. **Nomadic Computing.** An approach for interacting with technology, which emphasizes the need for continual connectivity. Connectivity is

achieved through body-worn computers, which are always on and always providing information to the user.

17. **Perceptual User Interface (PUI).** An interface that allows natural interactions with computers by engaging the human's cognitive, perceptual, motor, and communication systems and styles, and melding them with computational input/output devices that have perceptual and reasoning capabilities.

18. **Personal Digital Assistant (PDA).** A generic term for a pocket-sized, handheld computer that typically includes computing, telephone, fax, and networking capabilities. PDAs are often used as personal organizers keeping telephone numbers, addresses, and schedules handy.

19. **Smart Clothing.** A garment made out of computerized cloth that provides the wearer with various computational capabilities.

20. **Strong AI.** Simulating intelligent behaviors across a wide variety of problem domains. Goal is to create computers that think as a human does.

21. **Tangible Bits.** A vision of human-computer interaction that employs physical objects, surfaces, and spaces as tangible embodiments of digital information. These interfaces enhance human-computer interaction by associating familiar objects, noises, events, and activities with electronic information.

22. **Ubiquitous Computing.** Sometimes referred to as "calm computing," this term describes a work environment where computers are everywhere, and they are practically invisible.

23. **Virtual Reality.** An artificial reality based in three dimensions. A new (computer generated) reality replaces the actual physical environment in which an individual resides. VR is typically created via a head-mounted display immersing the wearer in a projected environment.

24. **Weak AI.** Simulating intelligent behaviors within a few precise, well-defined problem domains. The goal is to make computers do very specific yet useful things.

25. **WIMP.** A computer environment driven by *Windows, icons,* and *menus,* with various *point devices* available to the user.

S o, just what does the term *computer support* mean? In general, computer support involves goal-enabling technologies and their associated hardware, software, services, and techniques (Wilson, 1991). This interpretation is necessarily broad; more precise definitions are somewhat problematic because they become obsolete over time. In other words, computer support is not a static concept. As technology advances, so too does the particular meaning of these two words. This fact is exemplified by the transition from the million-dollar mainframe computer of the 1960s and 1970s, to the networked desktop PC of the 1980s and the handheld personal digital assistant (PDA) of the 1990s. Because today's computing trends will undoubtedly evolve as technology changes in the years to come, this chapter does not promote a specific, fixed description of computer support. Rather, it offers a snapshot of the current and emerging directions in workplace technology along with descriptions of specific applications to illustrate the latest computing trends.

This chapter focuses on three general computing trends: artificial intelligence, extended realities, and new interfaces or strategies for interacting with technology. We begin with a discussion of artificial intelligence and intelligent agents. Later sections address altered realities (e.g., virtual and augmented realities) that may be incorporated into various workplace innovations. Finally, current and forthcoming strategies for interacting with technology are described. These strategies involve ubiquitous computing, embedded multimodal interfaces, tangible bits, and nomadic computing technology.

## *Artificial Intelligence*

Perhaps no single topic has generated as much interest as the work in artificial intelligence. Just imagine a machine performing tasks much as does a typical worker or a worker with above average or superior capability. That seemed to be the promise of artificial intelligence many years ago. But what has happened to that promise—or was it a dream? Certainly advances have occurred in the area of making computers *smarter,* but have they really become the intelligent assistants that early researchers spoke of so brashly?

### Strong AI

Early workers in the area of artificial intelligence attempted to make a computer function much as does a typical adult. This early goal of having computers actually think as a human does is called strong AI. Some of the initial work began with machine translation of text from one language into another, such as Spanish to English. Early enthusiasm was high, and some initial, limited success occurred, but researchers rapidly came to realize that the problem was much more difficult than first believed. This is because early systems such as Newell and Simon's (1961) GPS program strove to model very general types of intelligence and intelligent behavior. Designing machines to exhibit truly *general* problem-solving behavior or intelligence, researchers discovered, is very difficult. In fact, it was impossible to have even the most sophisticated system demonstrate the type of common sense that is typical of a 6- or 7-year-old child.

One ongoing project includes the goal of developing strong AI, and that project is called CYC (rhymes with bike). The CYC project began in 1984 as a 10-year effort to bring commonsense reasoning to a computer (Lenat, 1995). The knowledge base in CYC contains concepts, facts, and rules—about a million total—and these are extensively and conceptually cross-referenced like a human's associative memory. CYC functions as an exhaustively cross-referenced encyclopedia using its concept-, rule-, and fact-filled knowledge base to reason. CYC has met a number of the goals that it set out to achieve, and more than many of the strong AI projects that preceded it.

Lenat and Guha (1994) provide various examples of applications that can capitalize on CYC's growing knowledge base. One example uses CYC as a basis for directed marketing. With directed marketing, product advertisements are tailored to each individual customer. A computer program can accomplish this goal by basing its marketing strategies on a customer's past history (e.g., previous purchases, school and employment records, banking transactions, etc.). Rather than simply recording these data, a CYC-based program can actually use the data, along with its reasoning capabilities, to make inferences about the customer's habits, lifestyle, interests, personality traits, areas of intelligence and irrationality, passions, and so on. With this information, the program can decide which product to offer the customer, and what argument will most effectively convince him or her to buy the product. A supermarket machine loaded with this type of software can readily print coupons tailored to individual customers who swipe their ID cards as they enter the store. Each customer's coupons discount products that he or she will probably consider buying, and they advertise the products in a manner that is especially appealing to the targeted individual. CYC is a necessary component of this application for a variety of reasons. First, it is very difficult to feed a wide range of customer data (e.g., habits, employment records, medical records, etc.) into a computer unless that machine is able to understand language, as CYC does. Moreover, persuasion involves a certain amount of savvy. Any good salesperson is able to size up a customer and choose a sales argument accordingly. This process involves reasoning capabilities that are not available in the nonintelligent technologies that preceded CYC. Additional CYC application examples are provided at www.cyc.com/tech-reports/act-cyc-407-91/act-cyc-407-91.html.

## Weak AI

After many early stumbles in the area of strong AI, scientists developed a focus on weak AI, which require computer programs to do very specific yet useful things. Researchers began to direct their systems to limited problems—problems in precise and well-defined domains. For example, a medical diagnostic system based on weak AI principles does not conduct *all* types of medical diagnosis; that is too large a problem for the program to handle. Rather, such a system assists with a particular area of medical diagnosis such as blood disorders. MYCIN was constructed as a diagnostic tool to help doctors in this diagnostic arena (Buchanan, 1984). Being very focused in its problem domain, MYCIN deviates from the general artificial intelligence, which characterized its strong AI predecessors. Instead, it features an expert-based version of artificial intelligence. In other words, it was designed to reason as would an expert in its specific field. In fact, MYCIN was built by extracting or mining the knowledge of many expert doctors. This knowledge was then codified into the system along with various representations of experts' problem-solving strategies.

Related to weak AI, terms such as *knowledge engineering* and *expert systems* stemmed from important work on systems such as MYCIN. *Knowledge engineering* refers to the process of extracting expert knowledge and encoding it for computer use. An *expert system* is a computer system that uses a database (or knowledge base) containing the knowledge and problem-solving heuristics of experts as well as control strategies that allow the computer to arrive at the same conclusions an expert would. An example involves extracting the knowledge from a doctor who is an expert in diagnosing blood diseases in children, codifying the knowledge, and placing it in a database.

Knowledge-based, weak AI systems have earned "a permanent and secure role in industry," and their current state is quite positive (Hayesroth & Jacobstein, 1994). In the workplace, expert systems will continue to serve in a variety of roles augmenting decision makers, planners, and those involved with many types of complex systems. Expert systems are available to assist strategic planning, financial models, and human resources management, to name a few examples. Scientists predict that the development of knowledge-based systems will continue to focus on expert problem solving within precise and well-defined domains. At the same time, advances in perceptual user interfaces (discussed later) will increase the ease with which these systems are able to communicate with users.

## Intelligent Agent Technology

The advance of intelligent agent technology represents additional progress in the domain of artificial intelligence. Although no universally accepted definition exists for the term *intelligent agent* (Milewski & Lewis, 1997; Sarma, 1996), a notion of what intelligent agent technology entails is agreed on. Broadly defined, an intelligent agent is a computer program that performs tasks without direct human supervision (Chen, Houston, Nunamaker, & Yen, 1996). An intelligent agent is considered an assistant or a helper rather than a conventional electronic tool (Lieberman, 1997). Conventional electronic tools require users to initiate all tasks and monitor all events (Maes, 1994). Intelligent agents, which are able to work autonomously and initiate tasks without being told to do so, are considered the opposite of direct-manipulation devices. Intelligent agents have been referred to as cousins of robots; like robots, they simulate human relationships by providing assistance that another person could otherwise offer (Bates, 1994; Sarma, 1996; Selker, 1994). In this regard, an intelligent agent has been likened to an English butler that performs tasks with a keen ability to perceive and attend to user needs (Negroponte, as cited in Selker, 1994). An example of an early, simple agent is the "office assistant" available to people using Microsoft Word and Excel. This assistant performs a number of tasks, such as correcting typos, capitalizing words, and automatically numbering itemized lists. The user does not *ask* the office assistant for this help; rather, the program monitors the user's activities and initiates assistance when it seems most appropriate.

Formal definitions of intelligent agents are necessarily broad. Anything specific engenders controversy among scholars and computer scientists, who continue to debate exactly what an intelligent agent is and is not. The Massachusetts Institute of Technology (MIT) Media Lab Symposium on Interface Agents recently concluded a one-day meeting on agents with a panel session in which no one could agree on what made a piece of software an intelligent agent (Greif, 1994). Magedanz (1995) notes that it is almost impossible to devise a sharp yet comprehensive definition for the term *intelligent agent*. Therefore, he suggests that it is more useful to identify the dominant characteristics of agent-based computing and then classify intelligent agent technology according to those characteristics. To this end, most definitions contain some combination of the following seven characteristics:

1. The ability to work asynchronously and autonomously without intervention from humans
2. The ability to change behavior according to accumulated knowledge, that is, the ability to *learn*
3. The ability to take initiative
4. Inferential capability (i.e., the ability to go beyond the user's concrete instructions and use symbolic abstraction to solve problems)
5. Prior knowledge of general goals and preferred methods
6. Natural language
7. Personality (Milewski & Lewis, 1997)

Different intelligent agents possess varying amounts of these seven characteristics.

Various complex, technical properties enable intelligent agents to function and exhibit many of the previously listed characteristics. This structural complexity may lead to the erroneous conclusion that intelligent agent assistance is designed for individuals with extensive computer knowledge. Although the architecture underlying intelligent agent technology is complex, the use of this technology is not. Agent-based applications are designed to solve a wide variety of technical and nontechnical problems for individuals possessing diverse levels of computer expertise (Milewski & Lewis, 1997). Roesler and Hawkins (1994) indicate that agent-based applications are ideal for the increasingly mobile workforce, because intelligent agents can filter and route messages to recipients on the move. Intelligent agent technology is also appropriate for untrained workers who are struggling with information and work overload (Maes, 1994). Additionally, all types of *knowledge workers* (e.g., managers, technical professionals, office personnel, etc.) may benefit from intelligent agent technology.

Intelligent agents can assist many different types of workers because this technology can be *attached* to a variety of applications. For example, intelligent agent technology can be applied to electronic tutoring systems, word processing programs, spreadsheet programs, Web browsing and search applications, supervisory control systems, visitor and meeting scheduling software, e-mail filtering systems, information retrieval systems, information filtering systems, travel arrangement tools, financial investment software, distributed decision support systems, electronic-meeting software, group problem-solving software, and other types of groupware and teamware (Bird, 1997; Bocionek, 1995; Chen et al., 1996; Connors, Harrison, & Summit, 1994; Coury & Semmel, 1996; Etzioni & Weld, 1995; Maes, 1994; Magedanz, 1995; Mitchell, Caruana, Freitag, McDermott, & Zabowski, 1994; Montazemi & Gupta, 1997; Riecken, 1994; Roesler & Hawkins, 1994; Sen, Haynes, & Arora, 1997).

Consider, for example, an intelligent agent's role in a meeting scheduling application (Bocionek, 1995; Sen et al., 1997). Agents involved in this type of software may demonstrate autonomous goal-directed behavior, the ability to infer, the ability to communicate with humans and other agents, and the ability to learn. Agent-based negotiation-and-scheduling software typically begins by assigning different agents to various team members. Each agent gathers information regarding its user's schedule and individual preferences, and it uses this information to negotiate and set up meetings for the user. For instance, suppose a worker named Fred generally prefers not to meet during lunchtime; however, he wishes to accommodate his team leader's meeting preferences whenever possible. In this case, the intelligent agent will avoid scheduling lunchtime meetings, agreeing to such meetings on Fred's behalf only when the team leader is involved. A scheduling agent's negotiations may occur via e-mail. Therefore, the agent can negotiate by exchanging messages with humans or with other users' agents. Furthermore, the agent is able to learn more and more about its user's preferences (and therefore improve its scheduling performance over time) by tracking and recording the user's electronic activities. For instance, suppose Fred usually prefers late afternoon meetings. Over the course of time the agent may schedule 10 different 4:00 p.m. meetings involving Fred and a teammate named Jessica. Further suppose that Fred manually deletes 8 of these 10 prearranged meetings, and he reschedules them for an earlier time. After tracking and recording these manual changes to the electronic calendar, the agent might infer that, although Fred usually favors late afternoon meetings, he prefers to meet with Jessica in the mornings. The agent can then adapt its future scheduling behavior according to this newly inferred rule. In a sense, the agent has *learned* to improve its performance.

## Extended Realities

Extended realities represent a second general trend in computer support. With this approach, the physical environment is replaced or enhanced with electronic images and objects. Two types of extended realities are currently receiving a great amount of attention: virtual reality and augmented reality.

### Virtual Reality

Virtual reality is concerned with creating an artificial reality that is based in three dimensions. A new (computer generated) reality replaces the actual physical environment in which an individual resides. Virtual reality is typically created via a head-mounted display, immersing the wearer in a projected environment. The interaction by the user with the virtual reality typically takes place via a data glove. A data glove measures the movements of an individual's fingers and hand joint, with sophisticated models also tracking the movement of the wrist and elbow. Recently, Wexelblat (1995) developed a system that attaches tracking devices to various parts of a user's body to collect data concerning body movement. This technology allows an individual to use empty-handed continuous gestures, like the gestures used in everyday life, to interact with objects in the virtual world.

Virtual reality systems were originally developed for training individuals on high-risk tasks such as an astronaut repairing a satellite in space. Today, many additional applications are in use. In the field of medicine, virtual reality systems are used for a variety of purposes (Rodger & Pendharkar, 2000; Zajtchuk & Satava, 1997) including surgical training (e.g., visualizing organs and practicing techniques), medical testing and simulation (e.g., placing a medic or surgeon in a virtual battlefield to practice triage), and in rehabilitation (e.g., a virtual environment that can be explored in a wheelchair). Another example simulation application allows users to drive a vehicle through different urban environments (Bayarri, Fernandez, & Perez, 1996). NASA uses virtual reality for many visualization tasks, including flying over a Martian landscape. In the business world, virtual reality systems are used to create environments for teleconferencing (Hann & Smith, 1996; Jackson, Taylor, & Winn, 1999) and to investigate prototype manufacturing systems (Yan & Ramaswamy, 1998).

## Augmented Reality

As noted, virtual reality *creates* a universe for an individual who wears a set of goggles and perhaps a data glove. Feiner, MacIntyre, and Seligmann (1993) argue that instead of wanting to block out the real world, as virtual reality does, we want to interact with our real surroundings in many situations. An augmented reality occurs when a virtual world is presented within the real world, thus *augmenting or enhancing* as opposed to *replacing* the physical world. This is accomplished by creating the illusion of transparency and by generating rays of light to form computer-generated *overlays*.

In a sense, augmented reality can be considered the diametric opposite of virtual systems. Whereas virtual reality creates a universe, augmented reality enriches the real world. Virtual reality excludes desks, offices, coworkers, and discussions around the drinking fountain or coffee machine. Anyone not wearing goggles and a data glove is not linked to the virtual reality system and is consequently excluded from the artificial environment (Weiser, 1991). Because augmented systems are part of the real-world environment, they do not isolate users in this manner.

One useful application of an augmented reality is the Digital Drawing Board developed by Mackay, Velay, Carter, Ma, and Pagani (1993). These authors argue that we will never get rid of paper (as in "the paperless office"), and that we are committed to working with it; so the issue becomes one of augmenting our ability to work with both paper and computers. In the system that Mackay and colleagues developed for graphical designers, the goal is to let designers work as they normally do with paper and layout boards yet still have the advantages of powerful computer aided design (CAD) systems. Working on a paperless, electronic drawing board that resides in a regular office, users can replicate, rotate, and project handwritten images, which can also be rendered in 3D. Using augmented reality, the Digital Drawing Board allows designers to have the advantages of both the traditional designer office and a 3D CAD system.

The Xerox DigitalDesk is another application designed to augment individuals in the workplace. Developers of the DigitalDesk argue that workers typically interact with documents in two different worlds, a paper world for "paper pushing" and an electronic world for "pixel pushing" (Wellner, 1993). Unfortunately, interaction in either of these two worlds prevents enjoying the benefits of operating in the other. For example, when one interacts in an electronic world, the advantage of applying natural skills that have been developed over a lifetime is lost. These skills include the use of one's fingers, arms, 3D vision, ears, and kinesthetic memory.

Once again, instead of creating a purely virtual world, the designers of the DigitalDesk do the opposite—they add the computer to the real world for the user and create a computer-augmented environment for paper. On the DigitalDesk, which really is a desk, papers obtain electronic properties and electronic objects gain physical properties; thus the advantages of both the physical and electronic worlds are retained in the augmented world.

The three important characteristics of the DigitalDesk are that (a) electronic images are projected down onto the desk and onto papers residing on the desk; (b) the system responds to interactions with pens and the user's bare fingers; and (c) the system can read paper documents placed on the desk. The DigitalDesk achieves these capabilities through a system of video cameras pointed down on the desk and an image-processing system connected to a knowledge base that can sense and interpret what the user is doing.

A simple application of the DigitalDesk is its use as a spreadsheet. Consider a situation in which a user has various sheets of paper with numbers on them, perhaps totals from different accounts. If the individual wants to enter separate numbers from each paper into the spreadsheet, he or she can easily do so by pointing to each number. The number (for example, $41,234.00) is then culled from the paper document and placed into the spreadsheet. Once in the spreadsheet, it can be further manipulated, and manipulations can occur on the fly, through the use of hand-gesture controls to the computer.

A related augmented reality application suitable for groups and teams is the Double DigitalDesk, which allows two users in separate locations to share their own physical desks, while each sees, edits, and writes on the other's paper documents (Wellner, 1993). Each DigitalDesk grabs images from its own physical desk and projects them onto the remote desk; so each user sees what is on both desks. As an example, say Bob places a piece of paper onto his desk; an image of that paper is also projected onto Carmen's desk, and vice versa. Each individual can draw with a real pen on both paper and electronic documents, and the other user will see those marks appear on her or his documents. Furthermore, each user's hand is projected along with hand motions, so the workers can also point to places on documents. Such a system has been used at EuroParc (Wellner, 1993).

Augmented reality would be useful in many jobs. A job involving technical machine repair provides a good example. As both the complexity of a machine and the richness of its technical detail increases, so too does the demand to display repair information in the most effective manner possible. Ideally, information should be exhibited in a way that is consistent with the technician's understanding of the repair task. (This understanding is often called the mental model or cognitive representation of the task.) This goal can be met by augmenting descriptions of the equipment's important features or by visually enhancing instructions for performing a physical task. More specifically, augmented reality can be used to generate a virtual world that overlays and complements the technician's view of the machine. In this case, the repair technician may wear a very small see-through head-mounted unit that has the capability of displaying an augmented view generated by computer. The unit may include a motion sensor that is used for determining where the technician is looking. This orients the augmented reality system allowing it to determine what information the technician needs to see. For example, as the worker looks through glasses displaying information from the computer to one eye, his or her view of the world is combined with an image from the computer-generated display, thereby enriching the type and amount of information available (Feiner et al., 1993).

The KARMA (Knowledge-based Augmented Reality for Maintenance Assistance) system provides a more specific example of how technology can augment a worker's reality during machine repair (Feiner et al., 1993; www. cs.columbia.edu/graphics/projects/karma/karma.html). KARMA is called *knowledge-based* because it includes a rule-based expert system that takes into account information about the worker, the task the worker is currently performing, changes that occur in the real world when the worker selects an image to project, and how to project the image. The KARMA system can be used for numerous jobs, including the explanation of simple laser printer maintenance to end-users. A person looking at a laser printer may see a number of different images, including the location and identity of the paper tray, the action of pulling out the paper tray, and the resulting change in the tray's state (all shown in virtual space and correctly oriented relative to the real laser printer). Figure 2.1 illustrates this view and action.

In short, augmented realities are especially useful for jobs where individuals are trained in the use of tools or have a general familiarity with a device needing repair yet are not experts in repair. Other office applications of this type of technology are clearly possible. Consider a stockbroker who is able to view a series of stock quotes, select one, and have a graphical display of its historic

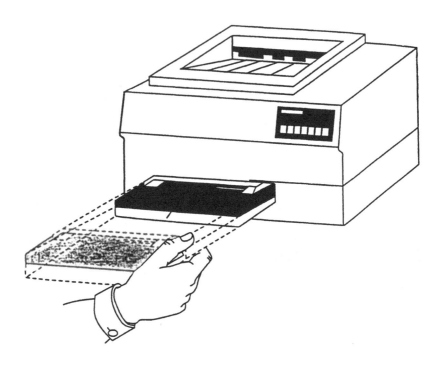

**Figure 2.1.** Augmented reality view showing the action of pulling out a paper tray on the laser printer and the resulting change in the tray's state.

SOURCE: Adapted from Feiner, MacIntyre, and Seligmann in A. Howard (Ed.), *The Changing Nature of Work.* Copyright © 1993 by Jossey-Bass. Reprinted by permission of Jossey-Bass, Inc., a subsidiary of John Wiley & Sons, Inc.

performance (or perhaps information about the company, e.g., Securities and Exchange Commission filings) overlaid on a computer screen. Consider also a surgeon who, during a spine fusion operation, has an overlaid model of a completed bone graft to refer to.

In the future, augmented reality systems will play an ever-increasing role in the workplace. These systems will be constructed around models of user abilities, accenting and enhancing their knowledge and skills. In this fashion, they will build on the strengths of individual workers, augmenting their ability to perform tasks of ever-increasing difficulty.

## *Interfaces/Strategies for Interacting With Technology*

The third general trend in computer support focuses on nontraditional approaches for interacting with technology. These approaches often employ creative new interfaces, and many depend on wireless technology, which is becoming an increasingly common alternative to *plug and play* hardware. This section discusses ubiquitous computing, embedded multimodal technologies, tangible bits, and nomadic computing.

### Ubiquitous Computing

Weiser (1991, 1993) and his group recently proposed one of the most provocative accounts of what office work will be in the future. The term *ubiquitous computing* (sometimes referred to as *calm computing*) has been offered to describe the work environment of the future. Computers will be literally everywhere; Weiser predicts that every office will have hundreds! Not only will they be everywhere, but they also will be invisible. The invisibility will come about for two reasons. First, many computers will be embedded into devices, the ceiling, and walls. These embedded computers will control both the environment and various office machines, such as the photocopier and answering machine (Elrod, Hall, Costanza, Dixon, & Des Rivieres, 1993). Second, the computers will be so commonplace that we will stop noticing them. That is, computers themselves will no longer be the focal point—something we have to deal with to accomplish a task. Rather, they will seem to disappear as they become increasingly prevalent and we take them for granted. Weiser describes the task of writing as an example of this phenomenon. No one focuses on writing in and of itself; it is a medium for working and communicating. We see writing all around us, in all aspects of our lives. Still, we do not focus on it; our focus is on what is being communicated. The same is true for answering a phone: We do not focus on the phone, we just use it. This phenomenon is similar to the notion of controlled versus automatic processing, which is well-known to psychologists. While learning a task such as driving a car, our attention is very controlled. After we are proficient at driving, however, we cease to be aware of each individual movement, and driving becomes automatic. A similar situation exists for professional basketball players. These athletes do not need to focus on dribbling the ball; they are free to concentrate on setting a play or making a move. In the coming era of ubiquitous or *calm* computing, the computers will disappear, and we will be free to focus on goals beyond how to use them.

The current downsizing of the technologies to laptops, notebooks, and palmtops is an example of the attempt to remove the computer from the focus of our work. What needs to happen next is for the computer to become a tool *through which* we work, and not the focus of our attention. Several ubiquitous innovations offer interfaces that allow technology to recede to the background of a user's attention. These innovations, which include the Xerox Tab, Pad, liveboard, Chameleon, and CHARADE systems, are described next.

Picture an icon that represents a file or folder on your computer. Now, imagine being able to pluck that icon off your monitor, put it in your pocket, walk to a separate office, place the icon onto a different monitor, and continue working with the electronic files in that folder. This is precisely how Tab technology works. Tabs, which exemplify the concept of ubiquitous computing, can serve a variety of purposes, but they primarily act as an information doorway (Weiser 1991, 1993). A Tab has a pressure-sensitive screen on top of a display and three buttons. Much as a common electronic desktop is organized on a Windows-based system with icons representing different information; Tabs can be dedicated to each project that an individual is working on. For example, a salesman might have a Tab for each sales account. Tabs essentially function as an extension of a computer screen. Instead of shrinking a window down, the information in the window can be shrunk down *into* the Tab. Tabs can be organized around a larger computer, and they are transportable, making it easy to take them from office to office. Gathering up information on a project is accomplished by gathering up the Tabs associated with the project. The programs and other files of interest can be called up on any computer.

An interesting application of a Tab is an active-badge system. As originally developed by Olivetti Research Labs, the active badge broadcasts the badge wearer's identification for automatic door opening in restricted areas (Hopper, Harter, & Blackie, 1993). Other features, which are implemented at the Xerox Palo Alto Research Center (Xerox PARC), include automatic call forwarding as badge wearers move about a building, customized computer displays for each individual, quick locating of individuals for a meeting, and monitoring the general activity of a building.

Moving up in physical size from the tiny Tabs are the larger Pads, which also provide ubiquitous support. Pads are a family of notebook-sized computers (not laptops or PCs), which are meant to be used much as one uses a piece of paper. Pads are intended to be picked up and easily used for any purpose. Personal digital assistants (PDAs) and the handheld computers used by traders on the floor of the American Stock Exchange are primitive examples of Pad systems

(Raghavan, 1993). The Crosspad is a full-function commercial product that evolved from the early Pad. It features a large memory, and it allows users to store information in a graphic format and convert handwritten notes into text for a word processor.

Much larger than Tabs and Pads are liveboards. Liveboards will serve many of the purposes of the white boards found in today's offices. They are wall-sized interaction devices with an area about 400 times the size of a Tab. Three current liveboard applications, TIVOLI, SLATE, and Magic Board (Crowley, Coutaz, & Berard, 2000; iihm.imag.fr/demos/magicboard/), support the cooperative interaction of several individuals working at the same time. The systems allow individuals to simultaneously work together on the same page or even on different pages of a project or report. Liveboards accept input in a variety of formats including pens, scanners, and gestures.

The Chameleon system is another noteworthy application (Fitzmaurice, 1993). Consistent with Weiser's (1991) conceptualization of ubiquitous computing, the Chameleon users interact with technology via computers that are embedded in the physical environment. By using a portable palmtop computer (approximately the size of a pager), the Chameleon system allows the worker to visualize, browse, and manipulate information in the 3D space. For example, a worker traveling to a branch office could use Chameleon to obtain information on weather, traffic, and points of interest merely by passing a handheld computer over a map and stopping where he or she wishes to receive information. In short, the Chameleon system, which blurs the boundary between electronic and physical environments, allows individuals to gain access to desired information without tying them to large fixed displays on their desktops.

CHARADE is another technology that represents a step toward making workplace computers ubiquitous (Baudel & Beaudouin-Lafon, 1993). With this system, a worker issues commands, not through a keyboard, voice, or pen but with freehand gestures. Consider an individual making a presentation in front of a group. Typically, the presenter will employ flip charts, slides, or some other medium. As the presenter goes through the information, he or she must typically pause and momentarily issue commands to the person controlling the projector. CHARADE gets around this awkwardness by allowing the presenter to issue commands (for example, "advance to the next page," "go back three pages," "return to the previous chapter," or "highlight a particular area") through the use of hand gestures.

As noted, ubiquitous computing is based on the notion that computers will recede into the user's attentional background. Hand gestures such as those employed with the CHARADE system promote such an environment for at least three reasons (Baudel & Beaudouin-Lafon, 1993). First, hand gestures are a natural form of communication. Second, they are terse and powerful—a single gesture can communicate quite a bit of information. Third, they allow a direct interaction with the device—the presenter's hand *is* the input device. CHARADE is implemented using a large display device that includes an *active area*. If 1 of 16 gesture commands (based on American Sign Language) is issued in this area, the computer interprets it, and the appropriate command is executed. Creating a presentation that is maximally flexible and seamless, this feature allows the audience and the presenter to focus on the presentation content rather than on the technology.

In addition to being an excellent device for presentations, CHARADE has been used to orient construction cranes and to conduct an orchestra of synthesizers, all through control by gesturing. Other applications include use in noisy office environments—individuals can communicate with one another and the computing system without interference from the noise. Finally, freehand input can improve the interactions of individuals who work in organizations where large displays are shared among many workers, such as those found in manufacturing plants, security services, and the stock exchange. In these office environments, freehand input can improve the manner in which individuals interact by allowing collaborative remote control of the shared devices (Baudel & Beaudouin-Lafon, 1993).

### Intelligent, Embedded, Multimodal Interfaces

By and large, the past 20 years have not witnessed significant advances in the manner in which everyday workers interact with computers. Graphical user interfaces still dominate the interaction dynamics, forcing individuals to type, point, or click through a series of windows, icons, and menus, with various point devices (the classic WIMP interface). In contrast, the computer supported cooperative workplace of the future may provide intelligent environments that are both embedded and multimodal, allowing truly natural human-computer interaction (Coen, 1998). According to this viewpoint, computer interfaces can be patterned after human interfaces. In other words, a computer with cameras for eyes, microphones for ears, and various sensing technologies can become an active, conversant partner in everyday life. It is important to recognize the distinction between ubiquitous computing and this intelligent, multimodal computational environment. Whereas the former is based on a *computers everywhere* philosophy, the latter maintains that we don't need computers and sensors embedded everywhere. Rather, a few embedded, intelligent devices with cameras and microphones can gather and communicate more information (e.g., the identity, gaze, and orientation of an employee) than can an active badge or a pressure sensor embedded in a chair, for instance.

This philosophy of interaction dynamics falls under the rubric of perceptual user interfaces (PUI) (Turk & Robertson, 2000). The goal of a PUI is to allow natural interactions with computers by engaging the human's cognitive, perceptual, motor, and communication systems and styles and melding them with computational input/output devices that have perception and reasoning capabilities. The PUI goal is accomplished by computers with perceptual interfaces that allow them to sense and to be aware of a user's hands, face, and body position. Some perceptual interfaces are even able to target how users feel and infer their affect accordingly (Picard, 2000). In short, perceptual interfaces help computers infer the user's intent as well as his or her actions.

Late-breaking multimodal interfaces (Oviatt & Cohen, 2000) promote the PUI objective by providing the user with a variety of computer input options. Input formats include combinations of speech, pen, and gesture, whereas multimedia output dynamics provide visual display, audio, and tactile (haptic) feedback. (*Haptic* is from the Greek word *haptein,* which means having to do with the sense of touch. See Tan (2000) for a brief overview of haptic interface issues.) A PUI integrates the perceptual interface, multimodal exchange between the user and the system, and multimedia applications (Turk & Robertson, 2000) to allow natural interactions. This integration is critical, because truly natural engagements among humans, technology, and work require CSCW tools (e.g., desktop, mobile, or embedded applications) that recognize and facilitate multiple interaction styles.

## Tangible Bits

Another exciting development is the work being done under the label of Tangible Bits. Tangible Bits (Ishii & Ulmer, 1997; tangible.www.media. mit.edu/groups) is a vision of human-computer interaction whereby the intangible bits of computer operations are made tangible. Consider for a moment those things that humans do well, such as sensing and manipulating the physical environment. Traditional graphical user interfaces use few of these skills. In contrast, *tangible user interfaces* employ physical objects, surfaces, and spaces as tangible embodiments of digital information. These interfaces enhance human-computer interaction by associating familiar objects, noises, events, and activities with electronic information. Associations are made both at the foreground and the background of human consciousness. Foreground interactions include graspable objects and electronically augmented surfaces, exploiting the human senses of touch and kinesthesia, thus leading to haptic interfaces. Background information displays use ambient media (e.g., ambient light, sound, airflow, and water movement). Ambient media communicates digitally mediated senses of activity and presence at the periphery of human awareness.

We briefly describe three tangible interface projects to provide a feel for the direction of this work. The first tangible interface is called *HandSCAPE* (Lee et al., 1999; tangible.www.media.mit.edu/groups/tangible/papers.html). HandSCAPE is a vectorizing digital tape measure used as an input for digitizing field measurements such as those taken in surveys, interior design, and storage space allocation. The tangible interface, which looks like a tape measure, uses embedded orientation-sensing hardware to capture relevant vectors on each measurement, and it transmits these data in real time via a wireless link to a remote computer. HandSCAPE provides seamless connectivity between the measured physical space and its digital representation while preserving the use of human senses and skills.

A second example of a tangible interface, called mediaBlocks, is based on small, electronically tagged wooden blocks (Ullmer, Glas, & Ishii, 1998; tangible.www.media.mit.edu/groups/tangible/projects.html). MediaBlocks serve as physical icons (termed *phicons*) for containing, transporting, and manipulating online media. The mediaBlocks interface works with various devices such as video cameras and projectors, allowing digital media to be moved (e.g., copied and pasted) between sources. The blocks permit direct control over the sequencing of media elements as well. As an example, suppose mediaBlocks A, B, and C represent a video clip, digitized image, and sound file, respectively. Physically placing the blocks in order B, C, A, will present the image first, followed by the sound file and then the video clip. Finally, mediaBlocks are compatible with GUI interfaces, thereby providing a seamless transition between graphical and tangible interfaces.

The third example is a project called TouchCounters (Yarin & Ishii, 1999; http://tangible.www.media.mit.edu/groups/tangible/projects/touchcounters/touchcounters.html), which are computational tags that follow and track the use of physical objects. Employing a variety of activity monitors, TouchCounters sense activity through magnetic, acceleration, and infrared sensors. Object status is indicated through bright LED displays. Magnetic snap connectors allow TouchCounters to be linked together and networked to a Web server, which generates a histogram indicating the usage frequency for each physical object (this process resembles the way a *hit counter* indicates the number of times a Web page has been accessed). Who would benefit from this type of technology? A manufacturer who needs to monitor the usage-life of assembly tools provides an example. TouchCounters could indicate how far into the life cycle any tool is. Another example is product developers who place alternative designs into a workspace—TouchCounters could monitor the actual usage of each alternative design. Tangible bit developments such as these will continue to allow workers to integrate natural interfaces into the world of work.

## Nomadic Computing

Nomadic computing is another fascinating approach for interacting with technology. The philosophy driving nomadic computing is that people need to be connected to computers continually—not just when they are at some home base, such as an office or a home computer. This connectivity is achieved through body-worn computers, which are always on and always providing information to the user. Advances in nomadic computing are made possible by recent developments in reducing the size of computational devices (see www.wearcomp.org/). Mann (1998) describes six key attributes of wearable computing:

1. *Unrestrictive to the user.* The wearable computer is ambulatory, mobile, and roving, allowing workers to do other things while using it. For example, one could jog while typing on a wearable computer.
2. *Unmonopolizing the user's attention.* The wearable computer does not cut the user off from the outside world as does a virtual reality game, for example. A worker can attend to other matters while using the apparatus. It is built with the assumption that computing will be a secondary activity rather than a primary focus of attention. It may mediate (augment, alter, or deliberately diminish) the sensory capabilities. Ideally, its mediation will enhance the senses in some way.
3. *Observable by the user.* The wearable computer can get the user's attention if he or she wants it to. It is *almost—always—observable.* Momentary lapses notwithstanding (e.g., a user might not see the screen while blinking or briefly looking away), the output medium is constantly perceptible by the wearer.
4. *Controllable by the user.* The wearable computer is responsive, allowing the user to grab control of it at any given time. Even in automated processes, the

come part of the loop whenever he or she desires. The desirability of computational control becomes obvious when, for example, an application mindlessly begins to open 50 documents that were highlighted when a user accidentally pressed *enter.* In this case, a large *HALT* button would give the user control over the computer. In short, the wearable computer is *infinitely—often—controllable.* The constancy of the user interface results from *almost—always—observability* and *infinitely—often—controllability* in the sense that manual override is possible but may not always be used.

5. *Attentive to the environment.* Wearable computers are environmentally aware, multimodal, and multi-sensory, ultimately increasing the user's situational awareness.

6. *Communicative to others.* A wearable can be used as a communication medium. It is expressive, affording the wearer the opportunity to be expressive through the medium, whether in direct communication with others or via the production of expressive media (artistic or otherwise).

Rhodes (1997) describes several additional characteristics of nomadic computing systems:

7. *Portable while operational.* According to Rhodes (1997), the most distinguishing feature of a wearable computing device is that it can be used while walking or otherwise moving around. This distinguishes wearables from both desktop and laptop computers.

8. *Hands-free use.* Military and industrial applications for wearables especially emphasize their hands-free aspect, creating the need for speech input and voice or *heads-up display* output (i.e., an electronically generated output of information superimposed on a user's forward field of view). Wearables might also use chording keyboards, dials, and joysticks to minimize hand interaction requirements.

9. *Sensors.* In addition to user inputs, a wearable should have sensors for the physical environment. Such sensors might include wireless communications, global positioning systems (GPS), cameras, or microphones.

10. *Proactive.* A wearable should be able to convey information to its user even when it is not actively being used. For example, if a worker receives a new e-mail message, his or her computer should be able to immediately communicate the arrival and the author of the e-mail, regardless of whether the worker was using the computer when the message arrived.

11. *Always on, always running.* By default, a wearable is always on and working, sensing, and acting. This contrasts with the normal use of a pen-based PDA, which typically sits in the user's pocket and is only awakened when a task needs to be completed.

Rhodes (1997; rhodes.www.media.mit.edu/people/rhodes/) has developed a nomadic system called the wearable Remembrance Agent. The Remembrance Agent is a system that continuously "watches over the shoulder" of the user of a wearable computer and displays summaries of information the wearer might find useful in the current context. Summaries include such items as notes files, old e-mail, papers, and other textual information that might be relevant to the user's current context. These summaries are listed among the bottom few lines of a heads-up display, so the wearer can read the information with a quick glance. To retrieve the entire text described in a summary line, the wearer hits a quick chord on a chording keyboard. (A chording keyboard allows users to press a series of keys simultaneously to input a word, much as they might play a chord on a piano or guitar.)

Most body-worn computers, such as the wearable Remembrance Agent, are battery operated, and in some instances, they are connected to a network via wireless technology. Some wearable computers are very observable whereas others are disguised and look like pieces of clothing or accessories. In fact, work is underway (Mann, 1996) to actually make the computer out of clothing. Two different strategies are being explored for the construction of *smart clothing*. An *additive* approach begins with ordinary cloth into which fine wires or conductive threads are sewn to achieve the desired paths for carrying current. Alternatively, a *subtractive* approach begins with conductive cloth and insulation for conductors. In this case, a desired pattern is achieved by removing certain portions of the insulation or by removing portions of the cloth itself. A simple application of smart clothing in an industrial or medical context would sense the wearer's alertness and stress level and provide feedback to the individual (Pentland, 2000).

The always-on and always-ready constancy of the nomadic interface can lead to a new form of synergy between the human and the computer. Although the computer is always on and always ready, computing is not the primary task of the wearer. The computer serves to augment the senses or intellect of the user. This approach is synergistic in the sense that each partner in the relationship is doing what he, she, or it does best. The computer does what it does best, thus reducing some of the demands on the human, thereby allowing the person to do what he or she does best.

Work in the area of nomadic computing is moving people from the point-and-click metaphor toward the look-and-think metaphor. In other words, mobile computing systems can function as a true visual memory prosthetic, which operates without conscious thought or effort. The human intellect is in the loop, and it remains a fail-safe mechanism for computers operating in the background. This synergistic relationship is different from other types of computer support such as environmental intelligence (e.g., ubiquitous computing). No guarantee exists that environmental intelligence will be present when needed or that it will be in the control of the user. Under the nomadic computing model, intelligent signal processing travels with the user. Furthermore, because of the close physical proximity to the user, the system is capable of a much richer, multidimensional information space than that obtainable by environmental intelligence.

## *Summary*

In sum, any definition of computer support must evolve as technology advances. Once tied to large, expensive, mainframe computers, this definition later changed to include networked desktop PCs and PDAs. In all likelihood, the future of computer support will move away from the desktop PC, toward more sophisticated and perhaps ubiquitous technologies.

Together, three computing trends (i.e., artificial intelligence, altered realities, and a movement toward natural or novel interfaces) illustrate some foreseeable directions in workplace technology, providing a better understanding of the contemporary meaning of the words *computer support.* The continued evolution of these two words promises exciting times for workers, organizations, and the field of CSCW.

# 3

# *Cooperative Work*

**Chapter Outline**
Work
Collaboration
Individual Work
Group Work
Teamwork
Organizational Objectives
Summary: The Relationships Among Technology, Multiple Levels of
Collaboration, and the Changing Work World

**Key Concepts**

1. **Cognitive Artifacts.** Codifying procedures and their resulting objects, which illustrate thought processes and make progress on cognitive projects visible.
2. **Cooperative Work.** Any work involving collaboration among humans.
3. **Group Work.** Activities performed by a collective unit of two or more people with a broad common goal. Group members interact with one another, yet their tasks are typically independent.
4. **Groupware.** A generic term for specialized computer aids (e.g., hardware, software, services) designed to support collaborative group work.
5. **Individual Work.** Activities that a single person performs alone.
6. **Organizational Objectives.** An organization's strategic emphases. The long-term and short-term goals embraced by the organization at large.

7. **Teamware.** A generic term for specialized computer aids (e.g., hardware, software, services, team process support) that are designed to support collaborative teamwork. Differs from groupware in terms of its ability to support interrelated interactions.

8. **Teamwork.** Activities performed by a set of two or more individuals who work interdependently and adaptively toward an organizational objective.

A good understanding of CSCW requires a reasonable grasp of the term *cooperative work*. To clarify the notion of cooperative work, we begin this chapter with a discussion of work in general. We then highlight fundamental differences among various types of cooperative endeavors and indicate that technology will facilitate collaboration most effectively when it is flexible enough to support the multiple, diverse levels of collaboration that occur within an organization.

## Work

The world of work does not exist in a vacuum. Rather, it is embedded in a political, economic, and societal context that nudges, constrains, and transforms it over time (Howard, 1995). This notion has implications for CSCW, for as the concept of work changes and advances, computer support must also progress.

Changes in the nature of work are perhaps best illustrated by briefly examining some of the evolutionary stages leading up to the information-rich, technologically enhanced work world of today. In contrast to work in today's environment, work in ancient times was primarily agricultural and was regarded as a loathsome drudgery. Ancient Greeks and Romans viewed work as the punishment of displeased gods, and ancient Hebrews considered it the price of original sin. During both the Renaissance and the Protestant Reformation, a more positive conceptualization of work (which was still mainly agricultural) was promoted. Following the Protestant Reformation, work was viewed as neither evil nor undesirable; rather, it was considered the mechanism through which rewards commensurate with personal efforts were distributed (Rue & Byars, 1980; Tilgher, 1977).

The industrial revolution, which began in Great Britain in the 1780s, shifted work away from agriculture and self-employment toward industry and the large organization (Rue & Byars, 1980). For the first time in history, agriculture did not employ a majority of the workforce. Rather, manufacturing and related employment, such as transportation, retail, and mining, dominated the labor market (Jones, 1995). Mechanized farm tools pushed people into the paid workforce where many demands for labor existed. Telegraphs, telephones, and railroads allowed firms to operate on a national scale. The appearance of electric power stimulated various technological innovations, including advances in the manufacturing process. Interchangeable parts gradually developed, promoting the division and specialization of labor as well as continuous-process assembly, which allows manufacturers to assemble products in a continuous fashion from start to finish (Howard, 1995).

Industrial employment began to decline in the United States after 1950, in Great Britain after 1951, in New Zealand after 1956, in Belgium after 1963, in France and Canada after 1964, in Australia and Sweden after 1965, in West Germany after 1968, and in Japan after 1970 (Jones, 1995). Following industrialization, advanced economies moved to a postindustrial service and information era. In other words, industrial employment was displaced by employment focusing on services such as welfare, education, administration, and the transfer of information (Jones, 1995). Although some scholars associate the advent of the personal computer with the postindustrial era, others consider the computer revolution to constitute a post-postindustrial era in and of itself (Howard, 1995; Jones, 1995). Regardless, today's advanced postindustrial work world is characterized by transportation and electronic communications that have condensed space and time, customer demand for flawless goods, reduced overhead, flatter hierarchies, an increasing reliance on teams, and high-tech industries where knowledge and human resources are prime sources of competitive advantage (Howard, 1995; Wilson, 1991, 1994). These trends, along with a number of additional changes, will continue to transform the workplace in the years to come. Fast-paced, global competition will become more and more commonplace. (According to Gwynne, 1992, only 7% of the U.S. economy was exposed to international competition in the 1960s, compared with more than 70% in the 1980s.) Industries will become increasingly service oriented; in other words, the shift from making a product to providing a service will be increasingly noticeable (Cascio, 1995; Kiechel & Sacha, 1993). Work processes will become more fluid and dynamic, and rapid workplace changes will cause organizations to abandon the concept of a *job* as a fixed bundle of tasks. Instead, organizations will focus on work *processes,* which are collections of activities that cut across job titles and organizational departments (Bridges, 1994; Cascio, 1995). Finally, organizations will outsource more and more of their work, decreasing the size of their overall workforces and increasing their reliance on contract workers.

In short, work has changed considerably, and it will continue to evolve in the years to come. It is important to note that although agricultural and industrial employment have declined over time, production within these areas has not dwindled; the need for humans among the agriculture, industry, and service sectors has simply shifted (Jones, 1995). As a result, jobs and the nature of work have undergone substantial transformations. [Incidentally, although the evolution of work has freed employees from a variety of workplace hazards (e.g., child labor and unsafe factory conditions), it is important to consider newer, subtler, health concerns, which emerge from modern forms of technology. Although this book does not focus on technology and associated health risks at work, we direct the interested reader to our chapter in the *Handbook of Occupational Health Psychology* (Coovert & Foster, in press), which addresses the topic in some detail.]

The preceding historical account illustrates the fact that work and technology exert reciprocal influences on each other. Technology serves to influence and transform work, and workplace changes drive the need for new technology. CSCW must remain attuned to the ever-changing climate of the work world, as this climate has implications for the development and use of technology in organizations.

## Collaboration

Just as work does not exist in a vacuum, neither does the worker who must accomplish it. Workers perform their jobs in the midst of, and often in conjunction with, other people. Different types of work require different forms and levels of cooperation, including individual, group, and team collaboration. Each level of cooperation possesses unique technological support requirements. Though far from trivial, the distinctions among these different levels are often overlooked by the field of CSCW, which tends to combine various forms of collaboration under the rubric of cooperative work. This tendency is probably one of the causes for CSCW's current confusion regarding the nature of cooperative behavior (Bannon & Schmidt, 1991; Scrivener & Clark, 1994).

It has been suggested that the term *cooperative work* must be clarified before the field of CSCW can adequately progress (Bannon & Schmidt, 1991). We support this contention and further maintain that the different levels of collaboration must be defined and distinguished before technology can appropriately support them. The remainder of this chapter addresses the multiple levels of cooperation that characterize the work world.

### Individual Work

Figure 3.1 portrays a globe that represents the world of work and its collaborative components. Individual work is depicted on the leftmost part of the globe. This type of work includes the activities that a single person performs while pursuing individual, group, team, or organizational objectives. Individual

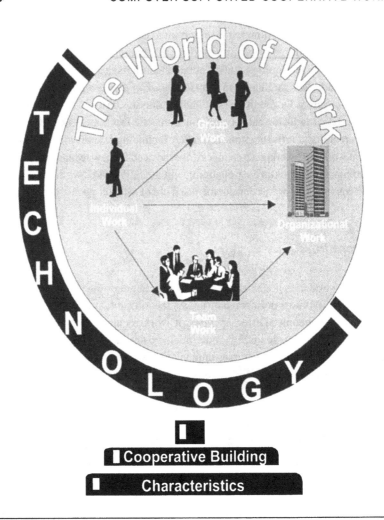

**Figure 3.1.** Technology must support multiple types of collaboration within the work world.

work is a critical component of CSCW because the modus operandi of individuals substantially affects the contributions they make to collaborative efforts (Wilson, 1994). From a technological perspective, the human factors involved in user interface design have important implications for individual work (Augustine & Coovert, 1991; Coovert, 1987, 1988, 1990; Coovert & Goldstein,

1980; Coovert, Salas, & Ramakrishna, 1992; Ellis, Gibbs, & Rein, 1991; LaLomia & Coovert, 1987, 1988, 1992). For example, during which types of input tasks are voice commands preferred over the use of a keyboard? Does an animated tutorial convey information more effectively than a text-based tutorial? Research addressing these types of questions contributes to effective CSCW by enhancing the quality of individual work. As Figure 3.1 suggests, individual efforts contribute to organizational functioning both directly and indirectly. A direct individual contribution occurs, for example, when a maintenance repairperson executes a set of unique tasks to fix a copy machine. Indirect contributions may occur via this individual's participation in group work or teamwork.

## Group Work

Groups and teams are two additional components of the world of work, and they are portrayed in the upper and lower middle portions of the globe depicted in Figure 3.1. A group is a collective unit of two or more people with a broad common goal. Group members interact with one another, yet their tasks are typically independent. People in groups may work at the same time in a common physical location or they may work at different times or in separate locations. In other words, time and space do not bind group membership. Two characteristics—interaction and shared goals—distinguish a group from a simple collection of people. For instance, the faculty within a university department form a group because these individuals share the goal of teaching students about a particular field of study and they interact with one another periodically. Conversely, all students within a university do not form a group because they do not all interact with one another and they do not all share the same goal (Spector, 2000).

A hospital maintenance department provides several additional work group examples. Within the context of the entire organization, the maintenance department can be viewed as a group that is separate from other units such as the accounting or the purchasing groups. Persons within the maintenance department may form smaller subgroups. For example, one subgroup within the maintenance department may be responsible for fixing office equipment. A different subgroup may be responsible for fixing medical equipment and yet another subgroup may be charged with structural maintenance of the heating system, air conditioning units, and so on. Within a group or a subgroup, members may communicate and share knowledge with one another, yet the completion of one group member's work does not directly depend on the activities of his or her colleagues. Salesclerks, security guards, and schoolteachers are also examples of group members who work in a relatively independent fashion but still come in contact with one another (Spector, 2000).

Work group members have much to gain from one another, and this benefit will likely occur to the extent that organizational technology facilitates the communication and informal interactions that allow group members to share information and to capitalize on one another's knowledge and skills. Such technology is typically known as groupware. Groupware, which can refer to hardware, software, and services, is a generic term for specialized computer aids that are designed to support collaborative group work (Johansen, 1988). Whereas some groupware technologies facilitate interactions among face-to-face coworkers, others support group members who are geographically dispersed. Furthermore, a groupware design can sometimes be adapted to both face-to-face and dispersed groups. The CHARADE system described in Chapter 2 is a good example of groupware designed to support face-to-face members. CHARADE facilitates group presentations by allowing a speaker to use freehand gestures to execute commands to a computer that stores and displays visual aids and other presentation materials. Standard, videoconferencing technology can be used as groupware to support dispersed members who wish to communicate. Finally, e-mail or electronic bulletin-board systems are types of groupware that offer support to both face-to-face and dispersed groups.

## Teamwork

Individuals working alone or within groups cannot effectively accomplish some types of work. Rather, many tasks require or benefit from a team effort. A team is a set of two or more individuals who work interdependently and adaptively toward an organizational objective (Cannon-Bowers & Salas, 1998). Realizing the benefits of teamwork, many organizations are currently reengineering work around teams' jobs rather than around individuals' jobs (Ilgen, 1999). As a result, teams are now used extensively in numerous settings, including factories, hospitals, schools, stores, the military, and other branches of government (Cannon-Bowers & Salas, 1998; Spector, 2000).

The distinction between groups and teams is worth emphasizing. Groups have long been studied by behavioral scientists, but teams have only recently come into the spotlight. Typically, groups are differentiated from teams in terms of task interdependence (Swezey & Salas, 1992). Whereas groups are collective units with little or no interdependence among individuals, teams have a high degree of interdependence, which necessitates interaction among members (Coovert, Craiger, & Cannon-Bowers, 1995). This distinction leads to different technological requirements for teams and groups. Namely, teams require computer support that facilitates task interdependence, whereas groups are less likely to require such intricate support.

Like groups, teams are not necessarily confined to common geographic locations and time schedules. Teammates can work interdependently from separate locations, and they can also work during different times of day. A few teamwork examples include airline crews consisting of pilots, copilots, flight attendants, and others, as well as new-product development teams consisting of various salespeople and service technicians (Cannon-Bowers & Salas, 1998). Effective teams can even form, for example, in a hospital maintenance department when a single person working alone cannot accomplish certain trouble-shooting and maintenance tasks that a team can take on successfully.

Coworkers in each of the preceding examples of a team require technology that will enable and facilitate interdependent interaction in the pursuit of common goals. Such interdependence is the defining characteristic of teams. Supportive technology, that can be labeled teamware, includes hardware, software, services, and team-process support (Johansen, 1988). Notably, teamware differs from groupware in terms of its ability to support interrelated interactions. In other words, interdependent individuals often reject traditional groupware because it ignores the interconnected features that distinguish teams from groups. Teamware allows coworkers to develop and maintain shared goals, shared understanding, and the coordination of cognitive and physical activities. In this regard, Hutchins (1995) suggests two important characteristics of teamware. The first is the support of cognitive artifacts that are in use by the team—that is, those codifying procedures that make projects (and progress on projects) visible. Secondly, teamware must support member behaviors in a manner that models the natural work practices of those individuals and also cues task coordination among individuals. Consider, for example, a 4-member team responsible for developing a customized product for a large organization. The members, who rely on their teammates' diverse areas of expertise, begin the task by developing two rough prototypes apiece, trading, critiquing, and building off each other's initial ideas. A large, adaptable chart, drawn on the whiteboard in the hallway, denotes who has submitted and critiqued which ideas. The chart, which is constantly updated as new ideas emerge and evolve, is an example of a cognitive artifact. Suppose each member of the team is transferred to a different office, and the four individuals, who now comprise a virtual team, must use teamware to complete a new project. According to Hutchins (1995), effective teamware will provide a feature that conveniently and naturally mirrors the team's cognitive artifacts (e.g., the hallway chart). Furthermore, the teamware will not require members to change the strategy (develop, trade, critique, and modify) that has worked well for them in the past, and it will prompt task coordination, which is easily lost in a virtual environment.

Like groupware, teamware can support face-to-face teamwork as well as dispersed teamwork. The Double DigitalDesk described in Chapter 2 provides a good teamware example. With this technology, two dispersed individuals share their desks, and they are able to see, edit, and write on each other's materials as the need arises. The Double DigitalDesk and other such teamware supports and even promotes interdependence.

Although many of today's commercially available technologies are reasonably well suited to individual and group work, few sufficiently support true team collaboration. Fortunately, it appears that upcoming technological advances, such as those illustrated in Chapter 2, will soon enable useful new systems that adequately support the intricacies of team interdependence. A number of upcoming cooperative teamware structures are introduced in the following chapter.

## Organizational Objectives

Organizational objectives are included in the rightmost portion of Figure 3.1. These refer to the organization's strategic emphases—the long-term and short-term goals embraced by the organization at large. In a hospital, for example, organizational objectives include the provision of safe and effective patient care. For any organization's objectives to be realized, multiple individuals, groups, and teams often perform a wide variety of functions. Broad organizational objectives will be facilitated to the extent that structural technology supports the functioning of diverse entities working at multiple levels of collaboration (individuals, groups, and teams) to achieve common overarching goals.

## *Summary: The Relationships Among Technology, Multiple Levels of Collaboration, and the Changing Work World*

In sum, CSCW should avoid treating work collaboration as a constant or changeless event. History has shown that just as technology transforms the nature of work, so must computer support adapt to an ever-changing work world. Today's increasing reliance on teams illustrates this point; new innovations are desperately needed because yesterday's workplace technologies do not adequately facilitate interdependent collaboration. As the concept of work continues to advance, computer support must simultaneously progress.

CSCW should also carefully attend to the multidimensional nature of work collaboration. Different types of work require different forms and levels of cooperation, as demonstrated in Figure 3.1's representation of the work world and its collaborative components. Although distinct, the different levels of collaboration are interrelated, not isolated. The arrows in Figure 3.1 signify the relationships among multiple levels of collaboration. Individual work contributes to organizational objectives both directly and indirectly via individuals' participation in groups and teams. Groups and teams, which consist of independent and interdependent individuals respectively, contribute directly to organizational goals. Many organizations depend on all three levels of collaboration. Moreover, individual workers often find themselves engaged in multiple levels of collaboration during the course of a single workday.

Technology, represented by the curved portion of Figure 3.1's globe stand, must support the dynamic world of work and each level of collaboration within it. Each type of cooperation has a unique set of technological requirements; therefore, it is important to make collaborative level distinctions during CSCW research and practice. This notion is consistent with the contention that CSCW is best conceived of as an endeavor to understand the characteristics of cooperative work with the objective of designing adequate computer support (Bannon & Schmidt, 1991).

The base of Figure 3.1's globe stand represents an organization's structural characteristics. This portion of the figure suggests that technology can successfully facilitate multiple levels of workplace collaboration only when it is supported by an appropriate structural foundation. Recent work in the area of *cooperative buildings,* described in the next chapter, highlights the importance of structural and environmental factors during CSCW.

# 4

# *CSCW Now and Later*

**Chapter Outline**

**Key Concepts**

1. **Adaptive Rooms.** Environments that dynamically adjust to workers' needs; include smart, digitally enhanced objects everywhere and are able continually to transform themselves to meet the physical needs and the cognitive work-flow requirements of their users.

2. **Cooperative Buildings.** Building-ware. Entire buildings constructed to facilitate and augment electronic and face-to-face communication and collaboration among humans.

3. **Covariance Structure Modeling.** A statistical technique that allows researchers to develop and test complex models that facilitate the investigation of directional (causal) and nondirectional (correlational or nonexistent) relationships among a wide variety of variables.

4. **Generate Tasks.** Team assignments that require members to generate as many ideas or solutions as possible.

5. **Intellective Tasks.** Team assignments that require members to find a demonstrably correct answer.

6. **Judgment Tasks.** Team assignments that do not have correct answers but do require members to seek consensus on a preferred alternative.

7. **Meta-Analysis.** A mathematical summary of the results of several different studies of a phenomenon.

8. **Negotiation Tasks.** Team assignments, often regarded as mixed-motive tasks, which require members to reconcile their conflicts of interest.

9. **Outcome Satisfaction.** Members' satisfaction with the final team product or decision.

10. **Participation Equalization.** A phenomenon that occurs when members contribute relatively equal amounts of input to a team conversation.

11. **Passive Objects.** Items that are assumed to remain unaffected by change; may be found in an adaptive room.

12. **Process Loss.** A decline in productivity caused by faulty team processes or interactions.

13. **Process Satisfaction.** Individuals' contentedness with team interactions that occur while members are devising decisions.

14. **Ranking Tasks.** Team assignments that require members to work together to place things in order.

15. **Reactive Objects.** Items that are able to self-transform, changing their position, orientation, or state not only in reaction to people but also in response to changes in other objects; may be found in an adaptive room.

16. **Team Conformity Pressures.** Pressure to express agreement with a team opinion; occurs when concerns for arriving at a unanimous conclusion override concerns for critical decision making.

As previously suggested, a proper discussion of CSCW requires an appreciation for both of its component parts—*CS* and *CW*. Chapter 2 described stimulating developments in the area of computer support (*CS*), and Chapter 3 reasoned that such technology will benefit organizations only to the extent that it facilitates each of the different types of cooperative work (*CW*) that occurs in an organization. The current chapter reunites the four letters, highlighting important characteristics of contemporary and future CSCW.

It can be argued that the overarching goal of CSCW is to promote effectiveness across multiple levels and types of collaborative work. To advance human effectiveness, technology must fully capitalize on people's strengths while diminishing their limitations. Progress toward such a lofty ambition is necessarily gradual. Although we continue to move toward this ideal as technology advances, many of today's CSCW technologies are somewhat deficient. Consider a traditional e-mail system, for example. E-mail effectively augments human limitations in many ways. It enables inexpensive, rapid, text-based communication, which was previously impossible to achieve. It allows people to communicate instantaneously, regardless of geographic and temporal constraints. Indeed, e-mail is useful because it compensates for some serious real-world restrictions. Although useful, e-mail is not ideal because it does not take full advantage of our natural strengths. As humans, we are able to communicate volumes via nonverbal signals such as posture, facial expressions, and vocal intonations. E-mail does not allow us to use these abilities. Better CSCW communication systems will not only reduce temporal and geographic restrictions, as e-mail does, but they will also allow people to capitalize on their nonverbal talents.

In general, current and future CSCW research efforts are grounded in attempts to (a) minimize users' limitations while maximizing their natural talents, and (b) understand users' reactions to real-world CSCW technologies, which are often imperfect. Though any such effort involves both technical and behavioral considerations, most CSCW research has either a behavioral or a technical thrust. For this reason, our description of CSCW's current and future directions begins from a behavioral slant and later moves to a technical perspective. Although behavioral and technical distinctions provide a useful organizational framework for our discussion, we remind the reader that the field of CSCW does not utterly segregate behavioral and technical issues. As previously noted, the interplay between the behavioral and technical elements makes CSCW unique and valuable (Wilson, 1994).

## Current Directions in Behavioral CSCW

Current behavioral research addresses human reactions to today's limited CSCW technologies. How do people react when new technological advantages are paired with unanticipated constraints? How do new technological enhancements affect intrapersonal and interpersonal processes? Recent research investigating the effects of computer-mediated communication and intelligent agent technology on team decision making exemplifies the type of work that is currently being conducted from a behavioral standpoint. These bodies of literature are discussed next.

### The Behavioral Effects of Traditional Computer-Mediated Communication Systems

Recent research suggests that text-based computer-mediated communication systems (e.g., e-mail) affect a number of team processes and outcomes. From a process standpoint, traditional computer-mediated communication appears to affect teamwork both negatively, by introducing new problems and deficiencies into the team process, and positively, by lessening the likelihood of certain team process losses. (A process loss is a decline in productivity caused by faulty team processes. For example, ineffective communication strategies that prevent a knowledgeable team member from sharing his or her expertise will ultimately suppress a team's productivity.) The previous assertion is substantiated by research specifically addressing the impact of computer-mediated communication on: participation equalization, team-member inhibitions, conformity for the sake of consensus, discussion comprehension, and decision-recording accuracy.

*Participation Equalization.* First, face-to-face and computer-mediated teams appear to differ in terms of participation equalization. A number of studies have revealed that computer-mediated team members tend to participate more equally than do face-to-face team members (Dubrovsky, Kiesler, & Sethna, 1991; Kiesler, Siegel, & McGuire, 1984; Kiesler & Sproull, 1992; McGuire, Kiesler, & Siegel, 1987; Siegel, Dubrovsky, Kiesler, & McGuire, 1986; Straus, 1996; Weisband, 1992). This equalization effect has emerged across numerous experimental settings varying in terms of team size (both 3-member and 4-member teams have been used), task type (both choice shift and ranking tasks have been used), and experimental participants (participants have ranged from undergraduate students to corporate managers to university administrators). The equalization effect is also supported by a meta-analysis (a mathematical summary of the results of several studies of the phenomenon), which tested the relationship between media type and participation equalization across six different studies (McLeod, 1992; Spector, 2000).

*Inhibitions and Controversy.* A second cross-media difference involves individual inhibitions and team controversy. Electronic communication media appear to reduce inhibitions and increase controversy among teammates (Dubrovsky et al., 1991; Kiesler et al., 1984; Siegel et al., 1986; Weisband, 1992). In this context, uninhibited behavior is typically measured by counting the number of remarks containing curses, insults, name calling, and hostile comments that occur during team discussions (Kiesler et al., 1984). This finding is not simply due to the anxiety that may stem from slow computer-mediated communication in the midst of time pressures. Indeed, computer-mediated team members appear to be particularly uninhibited, regardless of whether their task completion time is restricted (Walther, Anderson, & Park, 1994).

*Team Conformity.* A third difference between computer-mediated and face-to-face teams involves the extent to which members appear to feel pressured to conform for the sake of consensus. This pressure, which often arises during face-to-face teamwork, occurs when concerns for a unanimous conclusion override concerns for critical decision making (Janis, 1982; Maier, 1967). Research has shown that computer-mediated teams are less likely to reach consensus than face-to-face teams (Kiesler & Sproull, 1992), especially when they are inexperienced (Adrianson & Hjelmquist, 1991). This finding is consistent with the notion that computer-mediated team members experience little pressure to conform. Further evidence stems from the finding that face-to-face teams who are attempting to reach consensus require fewer voting rounds than do computer-mediated teams (Valacich & Schwenk, 1995). Additionally, third advocates (defined as the third member to publicly endorse a team decision) are significantly less likely to shift their opinions toward their teammates' proposals than they are when participating via computer (Weisband, 1992). Finally, research directly testing conformity supports the conclusion that computer-mediated team members are less likely than face-to-face members to submit to conformity pressures. Smilowitz, Compton, and Flint (1988) investigated this phenomenon by presenting Asch's classic "majority against a minority of one" situation to participants in an experimental computer-mediated setting. The participants were asked to determine the length of various lines while a computer program simulating four teammates (who were believed to be real) provided correct, slightly incorrect, or very incorrect judgments.

The results of this study revealed that the computer-mediated, simulated majority exerted less conformity pressure than Asch's (1956) face-to-face majority.

*Discussion Comprehension and Recording Accuracy.* A fourth cross-media difference involves interpersonal coordination. Several authors suggest that computer-mediated teams are especially likely to encounter general coordination difficulties. This notion is congruent with the empirical finding that computer-mediated teams are less likely to reach consensus than face-to-face teams (Kiesler & Sproull, 1992). Furthermore, compared with face-to-face individuals, computer-mediated team members have reported more difficulty understanding one another (Foster & Coovert, 2000a; Straus & McGrath, 1994). These difficulties could be due to a lack of informational feedback or a poor fit between the information-richness requirements of a task and the information-richness potential of the communication medium (Adrianson & Hjelmquist, 1991; Hollingshead, McGrath, & O'Connor, 1993; Kiesler, Siegel, & McGuire, 1984; Kiesler & Sproull, 1992).

Three recent studies on decision-recording accuracy coincide with the notion that computer-mediated teams experience coordination difficulties. In each study, face-to-face and computer-mediated team members discussed and devised collaborative decisions. Following team consensus, individual members recorded their teams' final decisions. When individuals participated in a face-to-face condition, they were much more likely to record the team's agreed-on decision accurately (Adrianson & Hjelmquist, 1991; Foster & Coovert, 2000a; Straus & McGrath, 1994).

Straus and McGrath (1994) examined the content of the computer-mediated teams' verbal protocols and found numerous instances when a team's transcriber recorded a team response with which one of the other members clearly disagreed. These authors suggested, therefore, that decision-recording inaccuracies stem from computer-mediated members' tendency to promote their own divergent opinions by deliberately misrepresenting their teams' decisions. Adrianson and Hjelmquist (1991) interpreted computer-mediated teams' decision-recording inaccuracies as an indication that these participants tend to develop confused or incorrect perceptions of the team's established decision. Although both explanations appear plausible, Foster and Coovert (2000a) found support only for the *confusion* hypothesis. Although team-discussion comprehension was statistically related to decision-recording accuracy, overall agreement with the team decision was not.

Moving beyond collaborative processes, it is important to consider the extent to which computer-mediated communication affects team outcome variables. Team performance, decision-making time, and member satisfaction are three team outcome variables typically addressed in the computer-mediated communication literature.

*Team Performance.* It is presently unclear whether the computer-mediated communication medium affects team task performance, because empirical results regarding this important outcome variable are somewhat inconsistent (Adrianson & Hjelmquist, 1991). A number of research studies have revealed that, during brainstorming sessions, large face-to-face teams produce fewer ideas than large computer-mediated teams (Gallupe, Bastianutti, & Cooper, 1991; Gallupe, Cooper, Grisé, & Bastianutti, 1994; Gallupe et al., 1992). Moreover, a meta-analysis of 10 studies concluded that computer-mediated teams using group support systems produce higher quality decisions than do face-to-face teams (McLeod, 1992). In contrast, several other studies have failed to find differences between face-to-face and computer-mediated team performance. This null result was obtained from teams working on both business cases (Adrianson & Hjelmquist, 1991; Archer, 1990) and ranking tasks, which require members to work together to place things in order (Adrianson & Hjelmquist, 1991; Straus, 1996). Straus and McGrath (1994) obtained the same null result from teams working on generative and intellective tasks. Generative tasks require team members to generate as many ideas or solutions as possible, and intellective tasks require team members to find a demonstrably correct answer. Alternatively, face-to-face teams outperformed computer-mediated teams on judgment tasks, which do not have correct answers but do require the team to seek consensus on a preferred alternative (Straus & McGrath, 1994). A similar study yielded slightly different results. Hollingshead et al. (1993) found no difference between face-to-face and computer-mediated team performance on generative and decision-making tasks. These authors defined decision-making tasks as those requiring team members to reach consensus when no solution is demonstrably correct. Furthermore, face-to-face teams outperformed computer-mediated teams on negotiation and intellective tasks. Negotiation tasks are defined as mixed motive tasks that require team members to reconcile their conflicts of interest. Hollingshead (1996) also reported no differences between face-to-face and computer-mediated teams who were instructed to select the best alternative among a set of choices. When she instructed teams to rank order the choices, however, face-to-face teams outperformed computer-mediated teams. Finally, McLeod et al. (1997) reported that face-to-face teams outperformed computer-mediated teams on a hidden profile decision task.

In short, the results regarding the impact of computer-mediated communication on team task performance are inconclusive. Valacich and Schwenk (1995) argue that these inconclusive findings might be the result of different research settings that have varied significantly in terms of team characteristics, tasks, and technological environments. Perhaps face-to-face and computer-mediated team performance differences depend on the extent to which a particular research setting (e.g., participants, task, technology) lends itself to various team process deficiencies. For instance, computer-mediated communication may be less advantageous when teams are already inclined to participate equally (irrespective of the medium) or when a task requires a particularly high degree of coordination of team members who are forced to work with groupware that does not adequately support interdependent behaviors.

*Time to Decision.* Regarding the time required to make a decision, computer-mediated teams tend to take longer than do face-to-face teams (Dubrovsky et al., 1991; Foster & Coovert, 1997; Hollingshead, 1996; Kiesler et al., 1984; Kiesler & Sproull, 1992; McGuire et al., 1987; Siegel et al., 1986; Straus, 1996; Weisband, 1992). At least two explanations for this difference come to mind. First, people typically type more slowly than they talk. Second, computer-mediated teams probably spend more time trying to coordinate their activities than do face-to-face teams.

*Process and Outcome Satisfaction.* In addition to decision-making time, traditional computer-mediated communication appears to affect team members' satisfaction. Several studies have revealed that face-to-face participants working on collaborative judgment tasks tend to be more satisfied than their computer-mediated counterparts (Adrianson & Hjelmquist, 1991; Foster & Coovert, 1997; Hollingshead et al., 1993; McLeod, 1992; Straus, 1996; Straus & McGrath, 1994). Although computer-mediated team satisfaction findings are fairly consistent, they often lack specificity (Olaniran, 1996). Indeed, *what* face-to-face teams are more satisfied with is not always clear. This ambiguity occurs because computer-mediated team satisfaction questionnaires tend to include a wide variety of items, such as satisfaction with the discussion, the process, the communication medium, and other members of the group.

Olaniran (1996) urges computer-mediated team researchers to abandon the vague *team satisfaction* construct and report specific types of satisfaction instead. In this regard, Olaniran offers the distinction between process and outcome satisfaction. Process satisfaction refers to individuals' contentedness with team interactions that occur while members are devising decisions. Outcome satisfaction refers to members' satisfaction with the final team product or decision. A few cross-media studies have investigated specific team process and satisfaction. One study revealed that face-to-face individuals working on collaborative judgment tasks generally feel more satisfied with the team process than do their computer-mediated counterparts (Straus, 1996). Another experiment measured both process and outcome satisfaction when investigating differences between face-to-face and computer-mediated teams (Foster & Coovert, 2000a). This study concluded that although face-to-face teams are more likely to feel satisfied with their collaborative processes, face-to-face and computer-mediated teams don't necessarily differ in terms of their satisfaction with the final decision.

   In summary, traditional computer-mediated communication systems appear to affect teamwork in important ways. The previous studies, which represent only a small subset of the research that has been conducted to date, address behavioral issues that are being empirically tackled by the CSCW community.

## The Behavioral Effects of Intelligent Agent Technology

   Another noteworthy program of behavioral research addresses the effects of intelligent agent technology on intrapersonal and interpersonal processes. As software designers and programmers continue to build intelligent agent assistance into their programs, computer-mediated groups and teams will increasingly include *nonhuman participants*. How do people react to nonhuman recommendations? Due to the relative newness of intelligent agent technology, this research area is not nearly as well developed as the topic previously described. Nonetheless, nonhuman participants are an important concern, especially because of the projected influx of intelligent agents into the workplace.

   One recent study compared intelligent agents and humans in terms of their relative influences over team decisions (Foster & Coovert, 2000b). The hypothesis was that intelligent agents influence their teams' decisions more than human participants do, and this influence occurs regardless of the agents' level of expertise. Thirty 4-person teams participated in a study designed to test this hypothesis. They worked on the Desert Survival Problem—a ranking task that required them to read a brief scenario and order 12 items according to their importance for survival to those stranded in the desert (Johnson & Johnson, 1994). This task, which is used in hundreds of organizations for training related to managerial decision making, has a single correct answer.

   Participants first performed the Desert Survival ranking individually and then reanalyzed the problem with their computer-mediated teammates. During the course of their work, teams used electronic bulletin-board communication software as well as a computer program that was believed to be an intelligent agent. The simulated agent possessed a cartoon-like anthropomorphic interface and used text-based natural language to communicate with the team. Approximately 15 minutes into the task, the "agent" recommended a solution for the team to consider. Teams were randomly assigned either a faulty agent or an expert agent, and the program provided poor and good recommendations respectively. Teams were allowed a maximum of 77 minutes to devise and submit a single, collaborative ranking of the 12 desert items.

Individual-solution quality scores were calculated and used to identify each team's best member. Specifically, a Desert Survival proficiency score was computed by first determining each human's individual-solution quality score (the absolute difference between a human's prediscussion ranking and the correct answer to the problem) and then subtracting the number of pretask desert-survival test items chosen correctly. (The pretask questionnaire included five multiple-choice desert-survival test items.) The human with the lowest desert-survival proficiency score was considered the team's best member. Influence scores were derived by computing the absolute difference between the team's collective, postdiscussion ranking and members' prediscussion individual rankings. Low-influence scores represented great amounts of influence. Influence scores were computed for both the intelligent agent and the best member within each team.

Best members and intelligent agents were compared in terms of their influence scores. The research hypothesis, which predicted that an intelligent agent would influence its team's final decision more than would the best human participant, was supported. Intelligent agents' influence scores were significantly better (lower) than the best human members' scores. Additional analyses did not reveal a main effect for agent-expertise level nor did the data produce an interaction between teammate type (human versus agent) and agent-expertise level (expert versus faulty), suggesting that the intelligent agent significantly influenced the team decision regardless of whether or not it offered good advice.

Qualitative analyses facilitated some interesting conclusions about team members' perceptions of their agent's influence. During the postsession debriefing period, the teams typically insisted that they paid little or no attention to the intelligent agent's recommendation. Indeed, a review of the electronic discussion transcripts indicated that teams spent very little time discussing the agent and its recommendations. Further content analyses suggested that the agent exerted influence in subtle ways, which probably prevented humans from realizing its effect. For example, the agent's suggestions appeared to influence some teams by giving certain members the confidence to express personal opinions that were consistent with the agent's recommendation. The agent seemed to influence other teams by lending credibility to members whose initial ideas were later reiterated by the agent. Thus, intelligent agents' influences are probably indirect and inconspicuous yet powerful.

In summary, today's behavioral research addresses human reactions to a wide variety of CSCW technologies. Traditional text-based computer-mediated communication systems and intelligent agents are two example technologies that are currently being investigated from a behavioral standpoint. The results of these types of research efforts provide insights into human reactions to new technological advances. Such insights form a foundation on which we can develop strategies for effectively managing workplace CSCW, and they also provide information necessary for improving present-day technologies.

## Future Directions in Behavioral CSCW

While CSCW researchers who have relevant expertise work to overcome today's technical deficiencies, behavioral scientists continue to investigate the effects of CSCW technologies on those who use them. How will people react to tomorrow's technological advantages? How will new technological enhancements affect intrapersonal and interpersonal processes? The broad issues will remain the same, yet the specific questions and answers will evolve with the technology.

It is important to note that today's empirical initiatives are occurring within a very young research area that is expected to mature as the field of CSCW progresses. To date, inclusive theories of the behavioral characteristics of CSCW are rare. Ideally, a wider variety of research and analytical tools will be used to promote broader theories of CSCW in the years to come. Specifically, future research should strive toward the goal of developing and testing richer models of the relationships among workers, technology, and the organization.

### Toward Models of the Impact of CSCW Technologies

Most of the findings described so far have focused on relatively simple relationships between technology and work. Although these simple independent and dependent variable designs are useful for gaining an understanding of the relationship between pairs of variables, the behavioral characteristics of CSCW are much more complex than these studies suggest. If we are to gauge the true impact of the changes brought about by CSCW technologies, researchers need to develop and test models that contain a rich set of the variables of interest and the relationships among them. These variables can be both exogenous and endogenous. Furthermore, they can serve not only as moderators but perhaps also as mediators of the relationships between variables. The relationships among variables in a technology-, job-, and outcome-model will probably take various forms. Some variables will have a directional influence on one or more of the other variables. Other relationships will be merely correlational in nature. Still other variables will neither influence nor covary with one or more variables in the model.

Advances in the application of covariance structure modeling will allow researchers to develop and test complex models of this type. These models may contain latent variables representing work, individual, or organizational constructs, with measured variables serving as indicators of those constructs (see Coovert, 1990, 1995; LaLomia & Coovert, 1989). This approach will allow us to test directional (causal) and nondirectional (correlational or nonexistent) relationships among a wide variety of variables.

In short, future CSCW research efforts must begin to move beyond today's simple theoretical snapshots depicting narrow relationships among people, technology, and the organization. Developing and testing models that express theoretically rich and meaningful relationships among our constructs is the only way we will ever be able to get a handle on the complex set of variables and their relations to one another. Only when we have developed models with rich explanatory power will organizations be in a position to effectively understand and manage the changes that are being brought about by CSCW technologies.

## *Current Directions in Technical CSCW*

As previously noted, the ideal CSCW technology fully capitalizes on individual, group, and team strengths while diminishing their respective weaknesses. The technical side of CSCW is currently gearing its research and development efforts toward overcoming the assorted hardware and software deficiencies that impede the realization of this ideal. Chapter 2 provides an elaboration of the current initiatives in the technical arena. These developments are being applied to individual, groupware, and teamware applications with varying levels of success.

The provision of adequate teamware is at the forefront of many technical research and development efforts. As previously suggested, *groupware* is just what its title implies—software that allows groups to capitalize on their strengths. Traditional groupware is often inappropriate for teams because it ignores the interdependent features that distinguish teams from groups. Teams require teamware, which differs from groupware in terms of its ability to support interrelated interactions. Although many of today's commercially available technologies are reasonably well suited to individual and group work, few sufficiently support true team collaboration. Thus, teams are forced to use groupware (which may explain why computer-mediated teams often feel dissatisfied with their collaborative processes). Fortunately, many current technical initiatives are focusing on ways to apply the technological advances described in Chapter 2 to support teamwork.

## Future Directions in Technical CSCW—Cooperative Buildings

In the future, the technical camp will continue to focus on the development of technologies that maximize individual, group, team, and organizational strengths while minimizing their weaknesses. Furthermore, the future promises a shift away from contemporary beliefs about how this ideal is best achieved. Researchers and practitioners appear to be moving toward an increasingly holistic view of CSCW. According to this new perspective, CSCW is not fully enabled by a single piece of technology, no matter how flawless. Rather, a broader organizational environment enables true and effective CSCW. This view is captured by recent work in the area of cooperative buildings.

Cooperative buildings, which represent a significant and late-breaking advance, are likely to play a major role in future CSCW. (The attributes of cooperative buildings are provided shortly.) This initiative is based on the notion that appropriate technology will foster successful CSCW only if it resides within a broader organizational environment that enables collaboration. The following work in the area of cooperative buildings describes the structural and technological characteristics of an organization designed to promote effective CSCW at *all* levels of collaboration.

## Building-Ware

Both interfaces and human-computer interactions have evolved in recent years, revealing a fascinating progression. First, simple interfaces operate at the command-line level. Significant advances were made with GUI (graphical user interfaces) and WIMP (Windows, Icons, Menu, Pointer; such as Microsoft Windows) environments. Then came room-ware, with the room itself serving as an interface to the computer (e.g., ambient rooms, ubiquitous computing). Body-wear makes nomadic computing possible. Finally, building-ware comprises entire cooperative buildings constructed to facilitate and augment communication and collaboration among humans.

A leading figure in the development of cooperative buildings proposes two goals for these structures (Streitz, Konomi, & Burkhardt, 1998). First, building-ware should support individuals and teams locally. As such, cooperative buildings must include on-site computing devices to assist people working alone or in teams. The second goal is to provide an environment that promotes the global cooperation of distributed individuals. Both goals are accomplished by identifying the appropriate work unit (e.g., individual, group, team, organization) and following the principles of user centered design to construct systems that support work at multiple levels of collaboration.

Cooperative building technology is also driven by the notion of multiple organizational *spaces.* To accomplish their work, individuals, groups, and teams must interact with various spaces within the organization, including the information space (communication and information technology), social space (work practices and organizational structure), cognitive space (tasks, job content, and cognitive processes), and the physical space (rooms, architecture, facility management). Cooperative buildings are designed to facilitate and augment work within each of these spaces.

## Future@Work

To exemplify the characteristics of a cooperative building, several companies recently pooled their resources and constructed a demonstration project called Future@Work (Hunt, Vanecko, & Poltrock, 1998). The Future@Work demonstration can be divided into two parts: (a) a modern building prototype that capitalizes on current computational capabilities, and (b) a conceptualization of the cooperative building of 2007 that takes advantage of the wireless technologies that will be available in the future.

*Modern Prototype.* The modern Future@Work prototype includes many noteworthy features. The conference area, for instance, includes soft indirect lighting to better support the use of multimedia and videoconferencing, a large conference table on wheels that breaks into smaller sections for use by breakout groups and teams, large multimedia cabinets built as furniture that can be moved and taken apart as demands on the conference room change, and finally, plenty of vertical spaces where information can be tacked onto walls.

Beyond the conference room, the building's broad architectural space contains highly mobile furniture, such as chairs, tables, and files that can be easily reconfigured to accommodate the preferences of any work team. Small personal spaces, owned by work teams, provide full privacy. Mobile, multipurpose partitions and screens serve as barriers that provide display and writing space. Totally adjustable ambient lighting and window treatments optimize preferences for light, and acoustic controls regulate white noise. Finally, large white boards are networked into the office infrastructure so that recorded information is easily disseminated throughout the organization.

*The Cooperative Building of the Year 2007.* The second half of the Future@Work exhibit provides a fascinating peek into the near future, predicting what the cooperative office and organization might look like in 2007. Specifically, wireless computing and communication technologies will untether those whose computational work activities currently tie them to the organization's on-site structure. Large interactive display devices will support collaboration within the office, and people will also perform complex individual and collaborative work from a variety of locations beyond the office. In other words, people will go to the office less often, and they will work away from the office more, reducing the percentage of workers in the building at any one time. Total quality of life will be an increasingly prominent issue faced by the designers of the future organization.

Village green is a particular space within the 2007 exhibit that typifies a large meeting area. The look and feel of the meeting space is similar to that of a hotel lobby; it is a common area designed to facilitate lively yet informal meetings. All of its furnishings are mobile, and the lighting is flexible. Wireless data communication technology is supported, and an authorized visitor can access information from the organization's network from anywhere within the village green by merely turning on a laptop computer. A large wall in the village green displays broadcast messages meant for the entire organization. This is easily viewed without dimming surrounding lights, and it can be used to display various computer-generated graphical information. Smaller group meeting areas are also provided in the green. In addition, private spaces allow individuals to work by themselves.

## Office VISION

Another intriguing vision of cooperative buildings is put forth by workers from the Danish Technological Institute. Their perspective, entitled office VISION, is an attempt to integrate four main themes within the working space: (a) sustainable working methods; (b) democratic organization; (c) a healthy indoor environment in which to work; and (d) liberating cooperative technologies to facilitate the ways in which humans work (Moltke & Anderson, 1998). These designers recognize that office work is embedded within a larger social context where activities are both formal and informal. While engaged in their ongoing work activities, workers continually communicate, supply information, and share materials or tools with their coworkers. Like village green, the Danish VISION recognizes the contingencies of cooperative work. In other words, cooperative work requires not only supportive information technology but also a supportive architecture that must provide an open, flexible, and dynamic space (real, augmented, and virtual) that will facilitate coordinated exchanges and support the social network throughout the workday.

According to office VISION, coworkers' communication must be natural and information-rich regardless of their physical proximity. Distributed coworkers must be allowed to communicate naturally by means of speech, facial expression, and body language. And the human must remain in focus during communication. These requirements highlight the traditional PC's inadequacy as a communication medium. In short, electronic communication should occur via an entire CSCW system that facilitates natural communication regardless of the user's distribution in space and time.

Office VISION promotes a holistic view of the worker within the surroundings. Moltke and Anderson (1998) are very much concerned with integrating living and working spaces into the environment. Furthermore, the environment itself must be both healthy and inspiring, thereby promoting wellness and productivity. To this end, Moltke and Anderson propose a wilderness area within the building that allows individuals the opportunity to experience a mysterious and exploratory environment—one that does not appear to have been made by humans. Similarly, indoor caves can also be provided by attaching a series of domes made of fiber-reinforced concrete. The domes are outwardly connected to the surroundings by large glass doors.

In addition to wilderness and caves, a sufficiently large patio should be provided to facilitate free activities. Open spaces, such as playgrounds and gardens, will also allow people to gather freely, and multimedia team spaces will provide liberating cooperative technologies. In short, the building structure envisioned by Moltke and Anderson (1998) promotes an *open office*, encouraging colleagues to learn from, interact, and teach one another. In this future workplace, cooperative work will be characterized by dynamic, flexible, and mobile interactions that are not yet supported by today's CSCW applications.

The success of a cooperative building is contingent on its acceptance throughout the organization's hierarchy. Fitzpatrick, Kaplan, and Parsowth (1998) described a project in which designers spent several years constructing a cooperative building in Australia. This story makes interesting reading, and the bottom line is that simply having the technology accessible is not enough. When those at managerial and organizational levels do not support the project, even the most advanced technological apparatus available can produce a cooperative building that is a dismal failure.

## Cooperative Rooms

In "A Room of Your Own . . .," Covi, Olson, and Rocco (1998) describe several additional points to consider when designing rooms in cooperative buildings. For example, team members using dedicated project rooms report several advantages when working in such facilities. These advantages include increased learning, motivation, and coordination. Cooperative-room designers should thus strive to create structures that promote these important aspects of teamwork.

Coordination is one of the biggest challenges encountered by teams. As suggested by the previously cited research on text-based computer-mediated communication systems, coordination becomes especially difficult when all individual team members are not physically located together. To be beneficial, cooperative rooms must support the coordination even of team members who are dispersed. This support should provide flexible, shared visual displays, and it should facilitate a convenient team-wide awareness of each member's activities.

Considering the typical types of support provided to individuals working in organizations, the cooperative room includes several common tools that are already in everyday use. For example, white boards, flip charts, phones, flow diagrams, transparency projectors, and computer projectors are available. Each is used in an organization to display information to individuals and teams. Organizations also display motivational tools. These include the company logo, the company's name on coffee mugs, and various inspirational messages spread throughout the work environment. A well-designed cooperative room will employ electronically enhanced versions of these common, everyday tools.

Today, many organizations also provide *war rooms* to support teamwork. A war room is designed to take advantage of physical space, strategically using it to facilitate teamwork. Under the appropriate conditions, having individuals work in close proximity with one another helps to promote motivation, inspiration, esprit de corps, and team effectiveness. The environment constructed by Ben Rich at Skunk Works exemplifies a war room (Rich, 1994). Engineers in Rich's Skunk Works often gathered diagrams that they were working on together and laid them out in the doorway between two different offices. This procedure increased individuals' ability to coordinate and work together. It facilitated an awareness of teammates' progress on the work, and it also constituted on-the-job training. Moreover, it smoothed the transition from individual work to teamwork and increased motivation among team members. Employees were likely to be inspired when they readily saw their teammates working hard.

An *adaptive room* is another cooperative structure intended to promote effective CSCW. Adaptive rooms are virtual environments that dynamically adjust to workers' needs. They represent an attempt to combine the best aspects of ubiquitous computing (the notion that computers should be everywhere) along with the insights of augmented reality (the idea that everyday objects can be digitally enhanced to carry information about their use). This technological synthesis yields rooms with smart, digitally enhanced objects everywhere—objects that may be passive, reactive, or active. Using such objects, adaptive rooms are able to transform themselves to meet the physical needs and the cognitive work-flow requirements of their users (Kirsch, 1998; also see Crowley, Coutaz, and Berard, 2000).

Advances in technology will enable organizations to adopt adaptive rooms in the not-so-distant future. Kirsh (1998) describes three lines along which an organization's adaptive rooms must conform. First, they must accommodate the various cognitive and physical work flows occurring within them. Second, they must attend to the social needs of users as they interact. Third, environmental coherence across room changes must be maintained; adaptive rooms are meant to be comfortable habitats. Consider the following scenario, which is based on Kirsch's work, as an example of how an adaptive room functions. Suppose an employee, whom we'll call Steve, is working alone on a project. He wants a certain configuration of papers on his desk. His desk is an appropriate size and shape, and his office walls hold bookshelves, pictures, and so forth. But when two of Steve's teammates enter his office to collaborate on a joint project, the configuration of his individual-physical work environment is no longer ideal. Because it is an adaptive room, the office transforms itself to facilitate the team experience. During this transformation, the bookshelves recede, the papers and digital information on Steve's desk fold into a 3D icon, and the white board on the wall expands to support collaborative exchanges. Furthermore, a small table in the corner of the office changes its dimensions to accommodate the needs of the team, and the ceiling lights automatically brighten and move toward the team's meeting table. After Steve's teammates leave and he is ready to return to his individual work, the office transforms itself back to the preferred mode for solitary work.

To make transformations possible, an adaptive office has sensors that register when a person enters the room. Suppose that Michelle, one of Steve's colleagues, leaves the team meeting early to work alone in a nearby adaptive office. After the nearby office recognizes Michelle's presence, it adjusts the lighting, temperature, music, and other aspects of the environment, based on her preferences. Later, as Michelle moves throughout the building, sensors interact with the telephone system, communicating her presence within the ubiquitous computing environment. Telephone calls are automatically routed to Michelle if she wishes to take them, or they are routed to her voice mail if she seeks privacy. This synchronization between the worker and the physical environment is achieved via explicit signaling among small, ubiquitous, computing devices that use digital information to detect people's positions as they move throughout the office environment.

For an intriguing description of an adaptive room built for children, see Bobick et al., 2000; http://vismod.www.media.mit.edu/vismod/demos/kidsroom/. The KidsRoom is a fully automated, interactive, narrative play space for children. It combines computer-vision action recognition with simultaneous computer control of images, video, music, light, sound, and narration to lead children through a storybook adventure. The system uses computational perception to keep activities in the physical space as children interact with virtual objects, scenes, and characters.

As suggested by the preceding examples, adaptive rooms are populated with both passive and reactive objects. Passive objects are assumed to remain unaffected by change. Reactive objects, on the other hand, can change their position, orientation, or state, not only in reaction to people but also in response to changes in other objects. Thus, reactive objects are able to self-transform, as illustrated by the bookshelves, papers, white board, table, lighting, and so on in the previous examples. In short, items of furniture found in adaptive rooms may be passive objects, such as traditional chairs, or they may be reactive objects, such as *smart furniture.*

Adaptive rooms are guided by three general principles. First, whenever possible, adaptive rooms should adjust to humans so humans do not have to adjust to their rooms. Second, adaptive rooms should be populated with cooperating smart objects and tools that digitally enhance the virtual environment to take full advantage of the principles of ubiquitous computing. Third, adaptive rooms should function as a system of distributed cognition. Problems should be solved by coordinating the resources of the individuals in the room and by maximizing the room's ability to facilitate collaborative problem solving for the team (Kirsch, 1998).

Incidentally, if adaptive rooms are ultimately to meet the cognitive workflow requirements of their users, a great deal of effort must be geared toward defining the cognitive components of work, which is a rather complex problem. Although job analysts (those who study and write detailed descriptions of jobs) can readily describe the objective or physical aspects of a job in terms of its tasks, duties, and so forth, the cognitive aspects of a job are much more difficult to express. Because a job analyst cannot observe the cognitive components of a job, he or she must make inferences as to their nature. Thus, if one wishes to construct an adaptive room that facilitates and augments the cognitive aspects of a job, careful attention must be paid to the problem of defining cognitive work flow.

In short, a holistic vision of CSCW contends that the simple provision of groupware or teamware does not guarantee effective CSCW behaviors. Rather, as the base portion of Figure 3.1 suggests, workers and technology must be supported by a physical structure that facilitates and augments communication and multiple levels of collaboration among humans. Current cooperative building prototypes exemplify such environments. Cooperative buildings (based on building-ware) may include features as simple as conference tables on wheels that separate into smaller sections for use by breakout groups. They may also entail more complex properties, such as indoor caves and smart, dynamic, adaptive rooms. Regardless of the details, a well-planned building will combine suitable technology—which enables individual work, group work, and teamwork—with a structural atmosphere that encourages collaboration, thereby promoting truly effective CSCW.

## Summary

Clearly, contemporary and future CSCW must be approached from both behavioral and technical viewpoints. Behavioral research initiatives help organizations describe, predict, manage, and enhance people's interactions with evolving technology. Technical research and development directly enables specific technologies that allow individuals, groups, and teams to capitalize on their strengths while minimizing the limitations inherent within different levels of collaboration. As the field of CSCW continues to mature, the interplay between the behavioral and technical initiatives will become increasingly important, bringing CSCW closer to the overarching goal of promoting effectiveness across multiple levels and types of collaborative work.

# 5

# *Human Resource Management in a CSCW Environment*

**Chapter Outline**

**Key Concepts**

1. **Affective Commitment.** A type of employee commitment that evolves from favorable experiences on the job. Occurs when employees wish to remain with an organization because of an emotional attachment.
2. **Autoinstruction.** A training technique that allows trainees to decide on the pace at which they receive and learn information.
3. **Autonomy.** The freedom employees have to do their jobs as they see fit.
4. **Behavioral Leadership Theory.** A leadership theory that examines the actual behaviors of effective leaders to determine what kinds of actions produce success.
5. **Behavior-Focused Scale.** A subjective performance appraisal instrument that concentrates on specific instances of behavior. These scales list behaviors that represent good and poor performance, and the rater indicates which behaviors are typical of the person being assessed.
6. **Comparative Rating Scale.** A subjective performance appraisal instrument that requires the rater to make some form of comparison between one worker's performance and the performance of other workers.
7. **Contingency Leadership Theory.** Suggests that leader effectiveness depends on a complex relationship between leadership style and a given situation; leadership traits and behaviors are not effective in all situations.
8. **Continuance Commitment.** Employee commitment that arises from a combination of investment in the job and the difficulty of obtaining another job; characterizes employees who remain with the organization because they need the benefits and salary or can't find another job.

9. **Effort.** The direction, intensity, and persistence of a human action.
10. **Employee Commitment.** A worker's attachment to his or her employing organization.
11. **Feedback.** Information about performance and how well employees do their jobs.
12. **Graphic Rating Scale.** A subjective performance appraisal instrument that requires ratings on several different dimensions. Each dimension includes a scale ranging from, for example, poor to outstanding.
13. **Growth Need Strength.** The need and desire for personal growth on the job; the desire to learn new things and develop new skills.
14. **Human Resource (HR).** The personnel or workers employed at an organization.
15. **Human Resource Management (HRM).** A set of interrelated processes involving the attraction, selection, retention, development, and use of workers to achieve organizational objectives.
16. **Job Analysis.** A systematic method for providing a detailed, snapshot description of a single worker's job in terms of duties, tasks, and responsibilities and of knowledge, skills, and abilities required to successfully perform the necessary functions.
17. **Job Satisfaction.** The extent to which employees like their jobs or aspect of their jobs.
18. **KSAO.** Knowledge, skills, abilities, and other characteristics. Human attributes, typically discussed in the context of HRM.
19. **Leadership.** An important HR function, which includes an individual's ability to influence the attitudes, beliefs, behaviors, and feelings of others in the workplace.
20. **Locus of Control.** The extent to which people believe they are in control of reinforcements in life. Belief in internal locus of control reflected in belief that one controls (through effort, skill, and so on) one's rewards in life. Belief in external locus of control reflected in convictions that luck, fate, or other people control one's reinforcements.
21. **Modeling and Role Playing.** Training techniques that require individuals to watch and imitate good job performance.
22. **Motivation.** A worker's willingness to put forth his or her best effort on the job.
23. **Negative Affectivity.** The tendency for an individual to experience negative emotions, such as depression, in many different situations.

24. **Normative Commitment.** A type of employee commitment that stems from employees' values and feelings of obligation. Occurs when employees believe they owe it to the organization to remain.

25. **Objective Performance Appraisal.** Use of hard, countable data to determine how well workers are doing their jobs.

26. **Performance Appraisal.** The formal procedures used to evaluate how well workers are doing their jobs.

27. **Performance Criterion.** A definition of *good job performance.* A benchmark against which a worker's job performance is compared during performance appraisal.

28. **Person-Job Fit.** An HRM concept that focuses on the assessment and attainment of a good *match* between the requirements of a job on the one hand and the talents and inclinations of a job holder on the other.

29. **Role Ambiguity.** A feeling of uncertainty about job functions and responsibilities.

30. **Role Conflict.** A sense of incompatible demands between two or more roles.

31. **Selection.** Choosing applicants to fill job openings. Scientific approach includes (a) using a job analysis to identify the most important characteristics of the job, (b) measuring the personal characteristics of numerous job applicants to determine the extent to which they match the requirements of the job, and (c) achieving person-job fit by choosing the applicant whose personal profile most closely corresponds to the job requirements.

32. **Simulation.** A training technique that allows trainees to practice task completion in an artificial environment that mimics the real job setting.

33. **Skill Variety.** The number of different skills necessary to do a job.

34. **Subjective Performance Appraisal.** Using judgments and subsequent ratings to determine how well workers are doing their jobs. Ratings are made by people who have observed the workers' job performance.

35. **Task Identity.** Whether or not an employee does an entire job or a piece of a job.

36. **Task Significance.** The impact a job has on other people.

37. **360-Degree Feedback.** A performance appraisal technique that provides ratings and feedback from multiple perspectives, including supervisors, peers, subordinates, and self.

38. **Training.** Teaching people to do jobs. Scientific approach to training involves (a) using a job analysis to identify the most important characteristics of the job, (b) measuring personal characteristics of current employees to determine the extent to which they match the requirements of the job, and (c) achieving person-job fit by teaching the necessary knowledge and skills to individuals who lack them.

39. **Training Evaluation Study.** A process designed to verify the utility of a training program. Specific criteria are typically examined in the context of a particular training evaluation design (pretest-posttest or control group with random assignment), which allows an organization to compare the performance of trained individuals with that of untrained individuals.

40. **Universalistic Leadership Theory.** A leadership theory that attempts to identify the major characteristic common to all effective leaders.

41. **Validation Study.** A process designed to verify the utility of potential selection tests or devices in the context of selection.

N ow more than ever, organizations must manage their human resources wisely. Because new job and worker requirements accompany CSCW, human resources (HR) managers will face many new challenges in the years to come. The trend toward CSCW is likely to exert unprecedented demands on various aspects of HR, including job analysis, employee recruitment and selection, training, performance appraisal, work motivation, job satisfaction, employee commitment, and leadership. This chapter addresses CSCW and its implications for human resources management (HRM), providing our perspective on what managers and those working with organizational personnel might encounter in a CSCW environment. Rather than offering an exhaustive treatment of HRM, we elaborate on several key areas, using a fictitious case study to discuss the ways in which CSCW may affect the future use of an organization's most precious resource.

## The Importance of HRM

HRM is a set of interrelated processes involving the attraction, selection, retention, development, and use of workers to achieve organizational objectives (Cascio, 1989). The potential effects of CSCW on HRM become particularly noteworthy when one considers the HR department's valuable role as a strategic partner in tomorrow's organization. HR is an essential component of any successful work organization. Indeed, some have convincingly argued that "if you want productivity and the financial reward that goes with it, you must treat your workers as your most important asset" (Peters & Waterman, 1982, p. 238). This concept will ring increasingly true in the years to come for two reasons. First, consumers and the ratios between labor supply and demand may change noticeably as the baby boomer generation retires and requires more goods and services. The key question will become not whether an organization can provide a product or service more cheaply than its competitor but whether it has enough of the right people to do it at all (Berwald & Hakel, 1999). Second, HRM will become more and more important as advanced economies continue to shift toward information- and service-oriented jobs. In such an environment, the quality of a product will not drive an organization's success; rather, the superiority of a company's human resources will be the primary source of competitive advantage. The quality of a workforce will become crucial in a world where almost every other factor that affects the production of goods or the delivery of services is available to every competitor. High technology, such as intelligent agents, will not provide an adequate substitute for a skillfully managed workforce in the future. On the contrary, such technology will make the workforce even more important for success (Cascio, 1995). In short, effective HRM is vital and will become increasingly essential in the years to come.

## The Current State of HRM

Industrial-organizational psychologists and various business specialists have spent a considerable amount of time and effort studying HRM and using scientific methods to develop and apply valid, effective solutions to HR problems. We now provide an overview of the current state of affairs. Specifically, we describe contemporary, scientifically based thinking on topics such as job analysis, selection, training, performance appraisal, work motivation, job satisfaction, employee commitment, and leadership. We invite the reader, while reviewing this HRM primer, to speculate on how these modern practices might change as we move to a work world characterized by CSCW.

### Person-Job Fit

Many current efforts have centered on the notion that workers must possess the knowledge, skills, and abilities that are necessary to perform their jobs successfully, and they must be motivated to use these talents effectively. Thus, modern HRM has focused on the assessment and attainment of a good *fit* between the requirements of a job on the one hand and the talents and inclinations of a jobholder on the other. As demonstrated in the following pages, job analysis, selection, training, and performance appraisal revolve around the realization of goals for the person-job fit.

### Job Analysis

In today's world, job analysis is a systematic method for providing a detailed, snapshot description of a single worker's job in terms of the duties, tasks, and responsibilities involved and in terms of the human knowledge, skills, and abilities required to successfully perform the necessary functions. The term *job analysis* refers to the tools and procedures used to collect job information as well as to the actual description that results from the data collection effort.

In terms of tools and procedures, many ways exist to conduct a job analysis, and no single approach is always best. Different job analysis tactics vary along at least three dimensions: the type of job data collected, the methods used to collect the data, and the individuals who supply the job data (Levine, 1983). Regarding the first dimension, multiple kinds of job information are available, and a job analyst must decide which type will best help him or her understand and depict the job of interest. Example data include descriptions of working conditions; the machines, tools, work aids, and equipment used on the job; workers' knowledge, skills, abilities, and other characteristics required to perform the job effectively; and the duties and tasks involved.

In addition to data type, job analysis procedures vary according to the methods used to collect job information: Job analysts differ in how they obtain their data. Possible information-gathering procedures include job observations, interviews of workers, opinion surveys administered to job experts, worker diaries, and reviews of workplace records.

The third and final dimension addresses the sources that supply job analysis data. Immediate supervisors, high level executives, job holders, technical experts, and customers can all provide information needed to accurately depict a job, and it is up to the job analyst to determine which sources are best in a given situation (Levine, 1983).

After collecting a great deal of data, job analysts produce a *snapshot* of the job of interest as it currently exists. This description typically includes the tasks, duties, responsibilities, and human characteristics that are required to perform the job effectively. Formal job analysis reports are the foundation on which many scientifically sound HRM processes rely. Levine (1983) notes that job analysis descriptions tend to serve three broad functions: HR development (training, recruiting, and selecting employees), HR planning (figuring out how many and what kinds of workers will be needed in the future), and HR use (developing performance-appraisal systems and redesigning jobs).

## Selection

Once a job has been measured via job analysis, person-job fit can be achieved through two different mechanisms—selection or training. The selection approach involves (a) using the job analysis to identify the most important characteristics of the job, (b) measuring the personal characteristics of numerous job applicants to determine the extent to which they match the requirements of the job, and (c) achieving person-job fit by choosing the applicant whose personal profile most closely corresponds to the job requirements. Numerous techniques have been developed for measuring knowledge, skills, abilities, and other characteristic (KSAOs), including assessment centers, work samples, interviews, and psychological tests (e.g., cognitive ability tests, psychomotor ability tests, achievement tests, personality tests, and integrity tests) (Spector, 2000). The best method for measuring applicants' traits depends on the nature of the KSAOs required by the job. Developing and choosing selection tests that accurately measure job applicants is a major undertaking that usually involves a validation study. Validation studies necessitate a series of important steps, including one that requires an organization to use the proposed selection device to assess a sample of employees who are not hired via the new test. These employees' test scores are correlated with their performance appraisals to determine the extent to which favorable scores on the selection device are related to high performance on the job. After these data have been collected and analyzed, the process should be repeated on a new sample of employees, to help verify the results of the first investigation.

## Training

In contrast with selection, training provides a different method for achieving person-job fit. The training approach involves (a) using the job analysis to identify the most important characteristics of the job, (b) measuring the personal characteristics of current employees to determine the extent to which they match the requirements of the job, and (c) achieving person-job fit by teaching or providing the necessary knowledge and skills to individuals who lack them. Although training is administered to both new and long-standing employees, most organizations spend the majority of the training budget on new employees. the necessary knowledge and skills have been provided, employees who are adequately suited to their jobs may or may not need ongoing or additional instruction.

The most effective training methods vary according to the nature of the job and the knowledge and skills that are to be taught. Many training techniques have been developed, and these often include methods such as autoinstruction (where training is self-paced), audiovisual and multimedia presentations, lectures, conferences, on-the-job training, simulations, and modeling, and role playing (where individuals develop knowledge and skills by watching and imitating good job performance). Designing and developing training programs that successfully teach and encourage individuals to use knowledge and skills appropriately is an important HR function. This undertaking typically involves a training evaluation study, which requires an organization to begin with a clear specification of the factors or criteria that are expected to change as a result of training. These criteria are usually examined in the context of a particular training evaluation design (e.g., pretest-posttest or control group with random assignment), which allows an organization to compare the performance of trained individuals with that of untrained individuals.

### Performance Appraisal

Regardless of whether the selection or the training approach is emphasized, person-job fit is assumed to be appropriate when an employee performs well. An accurate performance appraisal is necessary to determine whether an individual is working effectively; performance appraisal is thus an essential component of the person-job fit concept. The first step in developing an accurate performance appraisal system involves explicating the concept of *good performance* in the context of the important components of an individual's job. The essential job components (duties and tasks) can be derived from job analysis. After good performance in important job areas has been defined and performance criteria have been developed, an organization must decide how to assess an employee's current level of performance, to compare it with the criteria.

The many methods of employee evaluation include both objective approaches involving hard, countable data, and subjective approaches involving human judgment. Subjective methods are much more common than are objective alternatives (Spector, 2000). Subjective methods refer to ratings made by people who have observed a worker's job performance. A variety of subjective rating scales have been developed, such as comparative, graphic, and behavior-focused scales. Comparative rating scales involve some form of comparison of one worker's performance to the performance of other workers (Riggio, 1990). Graphic scales ask for ratings on a number of different dimensions, such as work quality and relevant personal characteristics. For each dimension, there is a scale ranging from *poor* to *outstanding,* for example. Finally, behavior-focused scales concentrate on specific instances of behavior. These forms list behaviors that represent good and poor performance, and the rater indicates which behaviors are typical of the person being assessed (Spector, 2000).

Many types of people are asked to use rating scales to assess employee performance. Although the direct supervisor is the most common rater, peers, customers, subordinates, or the employees themselves can also serve as raters of job performance. Indeed, several rating sources are sometimes used simultaneously, during, for example, 360-degree feedback. 360-degree feedback is a performance appraisal technique that provides ratings and feedback from multiple perspectives, including those of supervisors, peers, subordinates, and self (Spector, 2000). With 360-degree feedback, all raters do not necessarily evaluate identical sets of performance dimensions. Instead, a rater assesses only those dimensions that he or she is able to observe. Because people in different positions are privy to different aspects of an employee's job performance, multiple raters may increase the accuracy of a subjective performance evaluation.

After single-degree or 360-degree ratings have been completed, a knowledgeable individual provides feedback to the ratee regarding his or her current level of performance, and the organization makes a related assumption about the extent to which the employee *fits into* his or her job.

## Job Satisfaction

Job satisfaction refers to the extent to which employees like their jobs or various components thereof. Job satisfaction can be considered a global construct, or it can be discussed in terms of specific facets, such as satisfaction with pay, coworkers, supervision, and so on. Job satisfaction is usually measured via a paper-and-pencil self-report questionnaire. It can be accurately assessed to the extent that (a) employees are able to understand and recognize their feelings about the job, (b) they are willing to express those sentiments on paper, and (c) a reliable questionnaire is used. The Job Descriptive Index, Minnesota Satisfaction Questionnaire, Job Satisfaction Survey, and Job In General Scale are among today's most common job satisfaction questionnaires.

Job satisfaction is a complex phenomenon, and scientists have proposed numerous theories, which help explain what makes people like or dislike their jobs and what happens when they are satisfied or dissatisfied. Some theories suggest that job satisfaction will occur when the match is good between a worker's individual needs and the extent to which he or she feels the needs are met on the job. For example, according to this theory, workers who experience little freedom to complete job tasks as they see fit will experience low job satisfaction *if* they have a high need for autonomy.

Other theories suggest that aspects of a worker's role in the job or in the outside world lead to job satisfaction or dissatisfaction. Compared with their colleagues, those who are inclined to admit a sense of role ambiguity (a feeling of uncertainly regarding job functions and responsibilities) or role conflict (a sense of incompatible demands between two or more roles) are less likely to report satisfaction with their jobs.

Still other theories outline individual worker characteristics that may lead to job satisfaction. For instance, people with certain personality traits, such as negative affectivity and external locus of control, are less likely to report satisfaction with their jobs. Negative affectivity is the tendency for an individual to experience negative emotions (e.g., depression) in many different situations. Locus of control is the extent to which people believe they are in control of reinforcements in life. Although people with an internal locus of control tend to believe that they control the rewards in their life through effort, skill, and so on, those with an external locus of control typically believe that luck, fate, or other people control their reinforcements. Age also appears to be related to job satisfaction in that younger workers are typically less satisfied than are their older colleagues (Spector, 2000).

Finally, a fourth type of theory seeks to identify the specific job attributes that are connected with satisfaction. Hackman and Oldham's (1976) Job Characteristics Model exemplifies this type of theory. Illustrated in Figure 5.1, Job Characteristics Theory demonstrates how particular components of a job's design can ultimately affect job satisfaction and the other important work outcomes listed along the right-most portion of the figure.

According to the Job Characteristics Model, workers must experience three critical psychological states before they can achieve high satisfaction. The three critical psychological states are as follows. Employees must (a) perceive their work as meaningful, (b) associate a sense of responsibility with the job, and (c) have some knowledge of the results of their work-related efforts. The three critical psychological states occur to the extent that a job involves high levels of five core job characteristics (Spector, 2000):

1. Skill Variety: the number of different skills necessary to do a job.
2. Task Identity: whether or not an employee does an entire job or a piece of a job.
3. Task Significance: the impact a job has on other people.
4. Autonomy: the freedom employees have to do their jobs as they see fit.

5. Feedback: the extent to which it is obvious to employees that they are doing their jobs correctly.

It is important to note that Hackman and Oldham (1976) predict that the previous relationships among job components, psychological states, and work outcomes will hold only for employees who have a high degree of growth need strength. Growth need strength is the need and desire for personal growth on the job (Riggio, 1990), that is the desire to learn new things and develop new skills.

## Work Motivation

Motivation refers to a worker's willingness to put forth his or her best effort on the job. *Effort* can be defined in terms of direction (choosing one behavior over other possible actions), intensity (exertion offered), and persistence (task perseverance). Various motivational theories seek to explain individual differences in the willingness to exert effort in the workplace. Some theories suggest that people work hard to obtain rewards or attain goals. Other theories indicate that people exert effort to fulfill various needs. Still other theories predict that the very nature of a job can motivate people. In other words, employees will be motivated to perform work that is inherently interesting or otherwise enjoyable. Hackman and Oldham's (1976) job characteristics theory exemplifies this viewpoint. As previously described, the Job Characteristics Model predicts that employees with high growth needs strength will experience motivation and its associated psychological states when a job is characterized by skill variety, task identity, task significance, autonomy, and feedback.

## Employee Commitment

Employee commitment refers to a worker's attachment to his or her employing organization. According to Meyer, Allen, and Smith (1993), a person may have affective, continuance, and normative reasons for feeling attached to an organization. *Affective* commitment derives from favorable experiences on the job, and it occurs when employees wish to remain with an organization because of an emotional attachment. *Continuance* commitment arises from investments in the job or from a lack of employment alternatives. It exists when employees must remain with the organization because they need the benefits and salary or can't find another job. Finally, *normative* commitment stems from employees' values

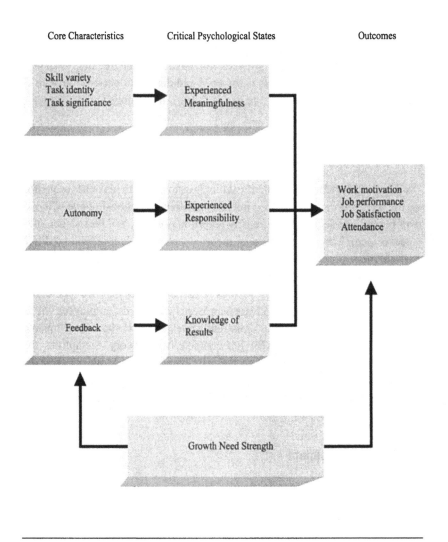

Figure 5.1. Hackman and Oldham's (1976) Job Characteristics Model outlines the job attributes that influence important variables, such as job satisfaction and work motivation.

SOURCE: Hackman and Oldham (1976). Used by permission.

and feelings of obligation. It occurs when employees believe they owe it to the organization to remain. Research has demonstrated a strong correlation ($r = .49$) between employee commitment and global job satisfaction (Mathieu & Zajac, 1990). Moreover, low commitment on each of the three types of attachments predicts leaving the job (Meyer et al., 1993; Spector, 2000).

## Leadership

Leadership is an important HR function that is characterized by the ability to influence the attitudes, beliefs, behaviors, and feelings of others in the workplace. Theories of leadership typically seek to answer the question, "What makes someone a good leader?" To the extent that an organization understands the answer to this question, it will be able to select the right people for leadership and train people in leadership positions

Theories of leadership can be characterized as universalistic, behavioral, or contingent. Universalistic theories typically attempt to identify the major characteristic common to all effective leaders, such as extroversion, dominance, or specific psychological adjustment (Riggio, 1990). Behavioral theories examine the actual behaviors of effective leaders to determine what kinds of actions lead to success. For example, a behavioral theory might propose that leaders who are high in consideration (who often express concern for the happiness and well-being of their subordinates) are more successful than leaders who do not demonstrate consideration behaviors. In general, universalistic and behavioral theories tend to be a bit too simplistic because they fail to recognize the need for diverse leadership styles in different situations. Contingency theories suggest that leader effectiveness depends on the complex interaction of leadership style and various situational characteristics. In other words, a single trait or behavior will not be effective in all situations. Contingency theories of leadership are currently the most popular, although a slight resurgence of interest in trait theory has recently occurred. Rather than focusing on conventional physical or personality traits, modern theorists are investigating attributes such as adaptability, which suggest that the ability to recognize and appropriately respond to changing conditions may render one an effective leader in many different settings.

In summary, contemporary areas of HR, such as job analysis, selection, training, and so on, are based on traditional assumptions about employees and the workplace. Many of these assumptions and practices will grow increasingly inappropriate in the years to come as we rapidly move toward a CSCW environment. Although one can predict the magnitude of CSCW's impending impact with some certainty, it is currently impossible to foresee exactly how it will affect the future of HRM. At this early point, we can only imagine the questions that managers and those working with organizational personnel may encounter in a CSCW environment. Perhaps this speculation best occurs in the form of a fictitious case study such as the one below, which provides a glimpse of HRM in the context of a typical insurance agent's job. The opening section describes a fictitious worker, the job, and associated HRM practices that exist today. The next section portrays the same worker 15 years later and shows the poor fit between modern HRM practices and the future CSCW workplace.

## 2001: A Case Study

### Al and the Nature of His Job

Consider the case of Al, a modern-day insurance agent working for a large U.S. organization that sells multiple types of insurance (automobile, health, life, etc.). Al is responsible for working in his community to market his company's products. His specific job duties involve identifying and contacting potential new clients within the community, selling insurance products to new policyholders, selling additional products to current customers, and providing professional insurance counseling to ensure the appropriateness of each policyholder's coverage.

Al is a full-time employee of the insurance company, he receives excellent benefits, and his company determines the products he sells. The completion of his job duties involves individual work, group work, and teamwork. For instance, he spends a portion of his time working individually to identify and contact potential new clients. After getting the names of local prospects from the phone book and the Internet, Al makes cold calls on the telephone. If he is unable to make contact after two attempts, Al asks the office secretary to mail a standard form letter that introduces Al and outlines the insurance services he provides. Incidentally, Al finds that the telephone call tends to draw more new business than the letter, and he reasons that perhaps the interactive nature of the telephone communication medium, which adds voice richness, has something to do with potential clients' positive responses.

If the initial introduction is successful, Al arranges to meet the potential client to discuss his or her insurance needs in more detail. Al meets the prospect either at his office or in the potential client's home, depending on the customer's preferences. Al likes to meet at the home—because his region is small, the drive is always manageable, and clients tend to be more relaxed and at ease in their own environment. Conversely, many potential customers prefer to meet at the office, and Al can certainly understand the safety concerns that arise when opening one's home to a stranger. Regardless of the meeting site, Al makes sure he has all necessary paperwork prepared for the initial visit, and if all goes well, he adds a new name to his list of clients before the meeting comes to a close.

Throughout the course of his week, Al occasionally engages in teamwork, collaborating with a variety of people for several different purposes. Consider the events that recently occurred when a client named Joe accidentally backed into another car in a grocery store parking lot. After completing the police report, Joe called Al to describe the events, and he faxed a copy of the police report to Al's office. Al then spoke to the crash victim and her insurance agent to learn the extent of the damage and describe Joe's coverage and the company's repair policies. Next, Al interacted with the appraiser, who met with both drivers and examined the wrecked cars closely. The appraiser assessed the damages on each car and estimated the repair costs. The appraiser worked closely with the automobile repair shop and an insurance claims clerk during this phase of the project. Eventually, the drivers took their cars to an automotive shop for repairs. Al and Joe then communicated with the claims clerk at the national insurance headquarters, and that office mailed a check to cover the repair costs. Al also spoke to the rates adjuster who computed Joe's new premium, which increased as a result of the wreck. In short, the insurance coverage of Joe's automotive accident involved Al in a highly interdependent team of consumers and specialists including the policyholder, the accident victim, the appraiser, the automobile repair shop employees, the claims clerk, and the rate adjuster.

In addition to individual and teamwork, Al's job also involves group collaboration. At his branch office, he works with six other agents, an office manager, and a secretary. Although Al and the other agents do not work together interdependently, they constitute a group because they share the common goal of promoting the company's product. Furthermore, they communicate periodically, assisting each other when they can. The town is divided into six comparable regions, and a region is assigned to each agent, who is primarily responsible for covering his or her own territory. The agents in Al's office typically share leads with one another, especially when a prospective new client resides within another agent's territory. Furthermore, the agents discuss new and upcoming court cases, laws, systems, and program developments that affect their jobs and the insurance offered by their organization. In fact, they recently set up an office bulletin board near the secretary's desk, where news clippings and other relevant pieces of information are posted.

In the context illustrated by Figure 3.1, Al contributes to the organizational objectives via his participation in individual work, group work, and teamwork. Although he uses his office PC to complete many of his individual tasks, he engages in group and team activities almost entirely through face-to-face or telephone encounters.

## Job Analysis and Selection

Al has worked for the company for several years, and he is quite good at his job. Indeed, scientifically based HR practices helped to ensure that Al and his colleagues are well suited to their jobs. In 1997, the national headquarters hired a group of industrial-organizational psychologists to conduct job analyses on each job within the company. During the analysis, the major job tasks and duties were identified as were the KSAOs required to perform them successfully. After the job analysis, the insurance firm revamped its selection system by building a set of paper-and-pencil tests, which adequately measured the most important andessential KSAOs for each job. (For Al's job, these tests targeted applicants' knowledge of insurance laws and sales techniques.) After validating the selection batteries, the organization began using the new tests to ensure a good fit between the characteristics of each employee and the requirements of the job.

## Training

The company also based their training program on the job analysis, and the program appears to be working well. New agents are sent to Atlanta, Georgia, for a week during which company training specialists teach them the necessary knowledge and skills that are typically deficient immediately after an agent is hired. The week in Atlanta involves lectures by trainers who discuss the company's policies and rules, as well as modeling and role play techniques during which the trainees watch trainers interact with fictitious clients and then imitate the trainers' behaviors. The company spends approximately 90% of its training budget on new employees. Thus, the Atlanta orientation is often the only formal job training that occurs during the course of an agent's career.

## Performance Appraisal

Al's performance is evaluated regularly, and his company recently implemented a 360-degree evaluation and feedback process. In other words, Al's performance is assessed by his supervisor (Donna, the office manager), his peers, several clients, and himself. A behavior-based paper-and-pencil rating scale is used in each case, and the raters evaluate Al on several different dimensions of job performance. For example, Al's supervisor rates him on how well he follows through with new leads, stays current on developments in the field, represents the company within the community, interacts with clients, and so on. Clients also rate Al on his interaction style as well as on how responsive he is to their needs and requests. Al and his peers rate additional performance dimensions plus some of the same dimensions assessed by the boss and the clients. The ratings are tallied and fed back to Al, who reviews them and devises a personal-development plan designed to improve his performance.

## Job Satisfaction and Motivation

Al enjoys his job quite a lot, and he believes he is providing a valuable service to the members of his local community. A recent company survey suggests that Al is not alone in this sentiment. According to the survey, both job satisfaction and motivation are quite high among the insurance agents in Al's group. As Felicia, the organizational survey manager, explained to Al and his group, these feelings of satisfaction and motivation appear directly related to the high degree of task significance that the agents associate with their jobs. "Task significance refers to the degree to which a job has an important impact on other people—either within the organization, such as coworkers, or outside the organization, such as clients" (Riggio, 1990), Felicia explained. Classic theories and subsequent research suggest that task significance is related to job satisfaction and motivation within a number of different jobs in Western countries (Hackman & Oldham, 1976; Spector, 2000). The reasoning is that workers experience greater meaningfulness at work when they believe their jobs affect others. According to Hackman and Oldham's (1976) Job Characteristics Theory, experienced meaningfulness directly relates to work motivation and job satisfaction, among other things.

## Employee Commitment

Al feels a strong sense of loyalty and commitment to the company for which he works. This is not surprising considering his high degree of job satisfaction and the strong correlation between global job satisfaction and employee commitment, which has been demonstrated in the research literature. In terms of commitment, Al experiences two types of attachment—affective and continuance. Not only does he have a strong emotional attachment to the company but he also simply cannot afford to lose the health benefits that his organization provides.

## Leadership

Al's supervisor, Donna, has been with the organization for 15 years, and she is an exceptional leader. The agents in the office enjoy following her lead, and they feel comfortable seeking her advice. Classic contingency theories indicate that effective leadership involves a complex interaction between a leader's characteristics and the characteristics of the relevant situation. Although Donna is not familiar with formal theories of leadership, she has spent a considerable amount of time analyzing the situational characteristics that arise with insurance personnel, and she knows how to handle the typical situations that occur. Over the years, she has effectively dealt with interpersonal conflicts, poor performance, promotions, and layoffs. According to Donna, only a few core problems or situations tend to arise, and she has an effective, well thought-out strategy for dealing with each circumstance.

Although she seems to be a natural, Donna has completed several leadership development courses, and she attributes much of her success to training, experience, and her former supervisor, who was an excellent role model. In her early days, any time Donna encountered a difficult situation, she simply reflected on the way her former supervisor would have handled it and acted accordingly. These days, Donna also reflects on the specific strategies taught in the organization's leadership training program. The organization based these strategies on a detailed analysis of critical incident-based insurance situations as well as on the employees that are typical within the industry.

## Traditional Techniques in a Changing World

In summary, Al's organization follows a typical HRM model that is based on past research and traditional assumptions of workers and work. But what happens when CSCW changes the nature of work and consequently invalidates our time-honored, underlying assumptions? The next case study, set 15 years in the future, highlights the arrival of CSCW, its sweeping implications for HRM, and the inappropriateness of modern practices in tomorrow's organization.

## *2016: The Case in Point*

### Person-Job Fit

"We really need to abandon this archaic notion of *person-job fit*" is a comment often heard these days. The year is 2016, CSCW is in full swing, and Al's organization is in trouble. Denise, the head of the HR department, is discussing the problem at the weekly department-head meeting. "In the past, person-job fit seemed a fairly reasonable goal," explains Denise. "From an HRM standpoint, scientists and practitioners always viewed each *person-job* as a distinct module, separate from other jobs and technologies. Unfortunately, this assumption is no longer valid now that collaboration in general and CSCW in specific have permeated the workplace."

"If person-job fit worked for us then, it should work for us now," the head of finance insists.

"Not really," argues Denise. "Twentieth century HRM was based on an individualistic view of the worker, and CSCW involves many kinds of cooperative relationships. Furthermore, in a CSCW environment, technology plays an active, independent, and frequently autonomous role in collaborative efforts—a role that the twentieth century HRM paradigm was never prepared to deal with. In short, historical HRM practices are not adequately guiding the effective management of today's CSCW workers because the person-job is just one component of a larger system, which actively involves other human and non-human associates."

## Al and the Nature of His Job

Fifteen years older and perhaps a bit wiser, Al overhears part of the conversation as he walks past the adaptive meeting room in the organization's cooperative building. Al still works as an insurance agent, and his job duties continue to involve identifying and contacting potential new clients, selling insurance products to new policyholders, selling add-on products to current customers, and providing professional insurance counseling to ensure the appropriateness of every policyholder's coverage. Although his general responsibilities remain the same, Al's day-to-day activities have changed considerably since he first began his job. Full-scale CSCW is now common, and a number of additional workplace changes occurred with the advent of this new computer supported collaborative work environment. Specifically, CSCW has developed within an atmosphere of rapidly changing, fluid jobs; an intense customer-service orientation; contract labor; and global competition. (See Chapter 3 for a discussion of probable workplace changes.) Al does not know whether CSCW caused, resulted from, or simply paralleled these additional workplace changes. In any event, his job has undoubtedly changed a lot over the last 15 years.

Al's company reorganized its structure in 2009 and converted all of its agents to *independent contractor* status. Thus, Al is no longer an official employee of the company, and he does not receive benefits. Overall, Al doesn't mind the arrangement, as he now earns higher commissions and has more freedom to run other businesses and sell additional products on the side.

Al currently works on a 10-member team that shares clients, territories, and even commissions. Five of the team members are human, and the remaining five are intelligent agents. The human team members are located in five very different locations throughout the world, and nearly all of their interactions are computer-mediated. Adequate CSCW technology (teamware) allows them to collaborate interdependently. Each human member on Al's team works closely with an intelligent agent *partner,* which is trained to perform certain team tasks autonomously in the absence of direct human supervision.

The organization encourages but does not require collaboration. Initially, Al didn't like the team concept, and he resisted the change. As other insurance agents moved to a team-based approach, however, Al found that he was losing business. A single individual simply cannot respond to a client's needs as quickly as can an effective team. Collectively, a team is immediately available nearly 24 hours a day—providing a level of customer service that an individual agent cannot possibly provide.

Though once exclusively domestic, the overarching company is now a multi-faceted international firm, which contracts insurance agents and provides a variety of additional services to clients all over the world. Some of these changes were made possible by significant advances in wireless video-conferencing technology, which replaced the traditional cellular phone years ago. These days, nearly everyone owns multiple *videophones* of various shapes and sizes, and the videophone is the primary method of communication. It is wireless, costs almost nothing to use, and puts people in (nearly) face-to-face, real-time contact with one another, no matter where they are located. Language barriers are partially resolved by intelligent agents, which readily translate one language to the next in real time, conveying not only the intended words but also maintaining the integrity of the speaker's voice.

Admittedly, the international aspects of the business have made Al's job a bit more challenging. Staying abreast of the changing insurance laws and procedures is much more complex than it once was, because the laws vary according to the country in which the client resides. Fortunately, one of Al's teammates is located in Europe and another in Asia. The human and nonhuman members of the team help each other remain current on new and impending litigation.

Overall, the completion of Al's job duties still involves individual work, group work, and teamwork. Nonetheless, Al finds that he performs less individual work and a lot more teamwork than he once did. In effect, many of the responsibilities that were once his alone have shifted to his intelligent agent or to the team. The intelligent agent performs the relatively mundane tasks that were previously individual endeavors. For example, Al rarely spends his time identifying potential new clients and making cold calls as he once did. Rather, he has trained his intelligent agent assistant to perform this task. The intelligent agent uses the videophone book and the Internet to identify potential new clients. The agent, with its image- and voice-reproduction capabilities, then calls potential clients on the videophone to advertise the team's products and services. The agent looks and sounds like Al during the presentation, yet it clearly communicates that it is indeed Al's software assistant and not Al himself. (International laws require this identification; Al and his team could be charged with fraud if the agent did not identify itself as a nonhuman entity.) The intelligent agent is able to call each videophone number repeatedly and tirelessly until it reaches the potential new client. Thus, the standard form letter that Al once used when he was unable to contact an individual is no longer needed. Al considers this a positive change, because the letter was never able to express the voice and interpersonal sales style in which he prides himself. By directly duplicating his image and voice, the agent effectively conveys the essence of Al, who has trained the agent to interactively field all but the most unusual questions.

When the intelligent software agent's introduction is successful, Al arranges to meet the potential client to discuss his or her insurance needs in more detail. Incidentally, the agent nearly has the expertise to complete a new policy from beginning to end; however, Al's team firmly believes in the importance of human contact early in the sales process. Although some of their competitors disagree, Al's team feels that this commitment to human interaction gives them a distinct competitive advantage. Al typically conducts the initial meeting via the videophone. From any location, he can meet clients—his virtual office travels with him. Clients usually prefer to meet from the comfort of their own homes, and Al views this arrangement favorably. He has access to all necessary information at his fingertips, and clients tend to be more relaxed and at ease in their own homes. If all goes well, Al adds a new name to his team's list of clients before the meeting comes to a close.

Various core insurance services continue to involve Al and his teammates in a larger team of highly interdependent consumers and specialists. For instance, when a client named Juan recently caused an automobile accident, Al's team worked closely with Juan as well as with the accident victim, the appraiser, the automobile repair shop employees, the claims clerk, and the rates adjuster. Although these individuals were in three different countries, they collaborated effectively to repair the damaged automobiles, provide the appropriate funds, and adjust the insurance rates as necessary. All of these activities occurred within a fraction of the time required to complete the same functions years ago.

Although Al's individual and team workloads have shifted somewhat, the volume of group work has remained about the same. For instance, Al still interacts periodically with other insurance agents outside of his team, usually at training conferences or via the videophone. Al values these group members because they are able to provide advice on useful new technologies and insurance sales tactics and techniques. Furthermore, Al interacts with various group members who work in his company's cooperative building. Although Al visits the physical work site approximately once per week, he enjoys his contact with the other people who work in the company's cooperative building. Interestingly, most of his physical coworkers are not insurance agents. The company continues to expand well beyond insurance, and it provides a variety of services (financial, legal, etc.) to its clients. Although they do not have a common specialization, Al and the group members in his building share the goal of promoting the company's products, and they use electronic bulletin boards to offer one another tips and pointers on providing state-of-the-art customer service.

Al thus performs his job within a high-tech, highly interdependent context. Because the organization has changed so rapidly, it is currently experiencing some difficulty managing its personnel within this CSCW environment. As Denise suggested at the department-head meeting, the general problem stems from a reliance on traditional HRM tools and practices, which are no longer effective in the new world of work.

## Job Analysis and Selection

In an attempt to stay current, Al's company completed a new set of job analyses in 2010, shortly after the first reorganization. During the analysis, the major job tasks and duties were updated along with the KSAOs required to perform them. After the job analysis, the company revamped its selection system by building a set of tests that adequately measured the most important and essential KSAOs for each job. They validated the selection batteries and began using them immediately to ensure a proper fit between the characteristics of each worker and the new requirements of the job. Initially, this approach seemed to make sense—it had served them well in the twentieth century. Because new technology and the world of work were evolving rapidly, however, the new 2010 job analyses were outdated by the time the company finished collecting the data to validate the selection tests. Somewhere along the line, jobs had become fluid, dynamic entities, and the company's traditional job analysis tools were designed to provide snapshot descriptions. In other words, the traditional procedures described static, unchanging jobs. By the year 2010, any effort to fit a person to a job via a *selection* approach resembled an attempt to hit a moving target. How can the company achieve person-job fit when the job keeps changing?

A related problem revolves around the *person* component of the person-job fit concept. Most modern jobs are team functions, not individual person functions. Thus, it seems that it would make more sense to fit a team to a function, rather than fitting a single person to a job. But how does one conduct a job analysis on a team? Furthermore, how can the company effectively select an entire team? Such problems seem to involve much more than a simple paper-and-pencil test assessing insurance knowledge, sales techniques, and a grasp of the latest CSCW technology. What kinds of people work well together? What makes a team function effectively? How should a company select a replacement team member after an individual quits, and how much authority should remaining teammates have during this selection process? Al's company is currently unsure of the answers to these questions, but they know they must identify solutions quickly if they are to make the most of their precious human resources. One thing they've noticed for sure—those employees who were not adaptable and willing to work in a team environment were not highly effective employees past the turn of the century.

## Training

The company recalls the day when it effectively based its training program on traditional job analysis and spent 90% of its meager training budget on new employees. These days, training is a well-funded top priority, and it is no longer reserved for new personnel. Long-term employees require frequent training to remain abreast of the new technology that continues to evolve. Indeed, rapidly changing technologies have increased the knowledge demands placed on all types of workers. Not only are they required to perform their jobs but they must also constantly learn the new technologies associated with their jobs. As a result, many individuals and teams have reported feeling increased pressure.

In addition to technological expertise, teamwork skills are essential in today's CSCW environment, and employees who lack them must learn them. The problem is, the company remains somewhat uncertain of what makes one team of highly competent individuals flounder while others work together effectively. Obviously, the company was unprepared for the full-fledged arrival of CSCW; prior to 2010, they had paid little attention to the characteristics and consequences of workplace collaboration.

Now in 2016, Al's company is beginning to recognize the importance of teamwork and training, and they are moving toward a continuous training paradigm. Training begins on the day a worker becomes associated with the organization, and it ends when the person terminates his or her relationship with the company. To deal with the pressures of increased knowledge demands, the organization adopted a *just-in-time* training philosophy—an outlook borrowed from just-in-time manufacturing. That is, the organization has decided to train only what workers need to know today (and perhaps tomorrow morning), while disregarding all other information until it is needed, and *never* training something that will never be used.

Of course, as independent contractors, the employees themselves are ultimately responsible for developing and maintaining their professional skills. Nevertheless, the company provides the training tools necessary to build the needed skills. Many of these tools involve self-paced, Web-based, collaborative autoinstruction technologies, which have replaced the traditional lectures and conferences. These new training technologies include intelligent, interactive, and augmented reality components—features that seem to facilitate learning much more than did the old training methods. Furthermore, workers are able to undergo joint and collaborative team training, regardless of the geographic distances that separate them. The company encourages personnel to seek this collaborative training, which teaches a variety of effective CSCW technology and teamwork skills. For example, Al's team recently completed a collaborative training module that focused on cross-cultural teamwork. (Although the intelligent agent components of the videophone are able to translate language in real time, they still cannot communicate the intended nuances involved in interpersonal communication. The cross-cultural CSCW training module taught the team to understand subtle yet important language and cultural differences when communicating with one another and their clients.)

## Performance Appraisal

Al's company continues to evaluate performance regularly, but they're in a bit of a quandary regarding which raters should evaluate which workers. Many personnel visit the physical work site once a month. Thus, those in the building are not necessarily in a position to observe the work performance of their office mates. Furthermore, questions arise about whether performance appraisals should be based on the individual or the team. The company also wonders how to account for the intelligent agents' influences. Everyone knows how compelling an agent's recommendation can be, even at a subconscious level. Should a well-meaning team be penalized for endorsing and following a faulty intelligent agent recommendation? Additionally, should individual and team appraisals be affected by the actual performance of the nonhuman participants? This question arose after a recent incident in which a team's software assistant began calling and disturbing clients late at night. The software agent's team claimed that the nonhuman teammate had malfunctioned, yet the company suspected that someone on the team had trained it to engage in this inappropriate behavior. The company recognizes the fact that they must change their traditional performance appraisal structure, yet they face a number of unanswered questions about the appropriate methods for doing so.

## Job Satisfaction and Motivation

Back in 2001, Al enjoyed his job because he believed he was providing a valuable service to the members of his local community. Now, he rarely services his local area; in fact, he does more business overseas than in his own country. The international component of his work has altered certain aspects of his job satisfaction and motivation. In the old days, he liked helping his neighbors, watching their lives progress, and getting to know the people around him. He loved unexpected encounters with clients in the local grocery store, at the barber shop, and in the mall. These days, he feels less and less connected to his clientele.

On the other hand, Al enjoys many of the new aspects of his job. He is grateful for the intelligent agent's assistance with relatively mundane tasks, such as searching for new clients in the phone book. He feels that this assistance allows him to focus on more important matters and to use a wider variety of skills on the job. In short, the nature of Al's job satisfaction and motivation have changed, perhaps in direct relation to a loss of task significance and an increase in skill variety (Hackman & Oldham, 1976).

Felicia, the organizational survey manager, is interested in measuring the job satisfaction and work motivation of Al and the others who promote the company's products. Yet she is not sure how to proceed with the assessment. Considering the major changes that have occurred in the world of work, Felicia questions whether classic theories of job satisfaction and work motivation provide adequate guidance. After all, these theories were largely based on traditional individual jobs, not team functions in multicultural CSCW environments. Felicia became particularly concerned with the applicability of classic theories after encountering a 1997 study by Pearson and Chong, which indicated that perhaps job characteristics such as skill variety and task significance do not lead to job satisfaction in non-Western societies. The literature further suggested that workplace relationships may be more important than job characteristics when determining satisfaction in Asian cultures, and the converse may be true for Western cultures (Spector, 2000). These concepts both intrigue and concern Felicia and the larger organization, which relies on Hackman and Oldham's (1976) classic job characteristics model to guide their examinations of satisfaction and motivation among numerous multicultural teams of CSCW workers.

## Employee Commitment

Al's transition to independent contractor status definitely changed the commitment he felt to his organization. Although he still feels some degree of emotional attachment or affective commitment to the organization whose product he promotes, continuance commitment no longer binds him to this company. In the old days, Al's health benefits were one of the major factors tying him to the organization. Today, his health benefits do not come from the organization; rather, he is in charge of this aspect of his life, and these benefits will travel with him if he decides to leave the company.

## Leadership

Al's supervisor, Donna, left the organization several years ago. In truth, she was having a difficult time adapting to the new work environment. Suddenly, she was encountering circumstances that she had never imagined, and she didn't know how to lead effectively in these new situations. For instance, shortly before she left, an outgoing employee insisted that he should either take his intelligent assistant with him or erase all data from the machine. The former employee claimed that he had trained the agent, and the data was thus his. Although Donna knew that much of the data belonged to the organization, she didn't know how to traverse this uncharted territory. Additionally, Donna had little experience facilitating teamwork, and this issue seemed to demand more and more time during her final months on the job. She was also unsure of the level of guidance she should provide virtual subordinates, whom she felt she hardly knew. Donna was certain that her former mentor had never encountered these types of situations on the job. She felt ill-prepared for the new leadership dilemmas, and she didn't know where to go for help.

After Donna's departure, the organization became much flatter. Self-managed work teams are now taking on more and more managerial responsibilities, and they do not need formal supervisors. Still, a handful of supervisors and other leaders remain necessary, and Al's organization recognizes the need to train them to lead effectively in an environment where they rarely experience face-to-face contact with their subordinates. They do not want to continue to lose good employees like Donna. Knowing that effective leadership involves the ability to influence the attitudes, beliefs, behaviors, and feelings of others in the workplace, the organization wonders how a virtual leader might best influence his or her subordinates? What leadership skills are most essential in a rapidly changing CSCW environment? How does one lead CSCW workers, who perform previously nonexistent tasks and rely on a set of brand new, constantly changing skills? A fast-paced, networked, interdependent CSCW work organization needs transformational leaders more than ever before (Bass, 1985), and Al's company is actively seeking methods for finding and developing such individuals.

## *Summary*

In summary, a typical HRM model that is based on traditional assumptions of workers and work leaves many questions unanswered for those attempting to effectively manage CSCW personnel. Al's organization was relatively unprepared for the advent of CSCW, and they were forced to simply react to the world around them in hopes of stumbling on effective HRM practices and techniques.

On a more positive note, future HR managers will have some amazing new tools at their disposal. Recall for example the self-paced, Web-based, collaborative team-teaching modules, which the training department in Al's organization adopted. High-tech training tools (e.g., intelligent, interactive, augmented reality simulations) can lead to significant advances in workplace learning, thereby facilitating effective HRM. If used wisely, future tools can initiate exciting, unprecedented improvements in various areas of HRM.

# 6

# *Concluding Remarks*

The world of work is changing faster than ever before, and we are rapidly approaching the *Age of CSCW*. Multiple levels of workplace collaboration (individual, group, and team) now characterize the modern organization. Each level possesses unique technological requirements that are being fulfilled by advances in artificial intelligence, interfaces, extended realities, cooperative buildings, and other technologies.

All signs suggest that we have seen only the tip of the CSCW iceberg. We must, therefore, begin to consider carefully how the shift toward computer-supported collaboration will affect the behavior and management of humans in the workplace. Clearly, current human resource management (HRM) practices will be inappropriate in tomorrow's CSCW environment. This book is designed to provide a springboard for consideration of the types of changes that must occur if we expect to make the most of (and do the best for) the people who collectively will form the future organization's most important asset.

Sweeping recommendations on how to manage high-tech CSCW workers would be premature; such advice must be based on careful and systematic research that focuses on effectively revamping our current practices to accommodate a rapidly changing work world containing many virtual and collaborative components. An applied research agenda of this nature will provide valuable HRM tools and techniques to the extent that both scientists and practitioners cooperate in its realization. Formulating effective solutions for today's changing world of work will prevent a dangerously reactive approach to HRM when CSCW becomes more commonplace.

Some observers suggest that the field of CSCW is best viewed as a community that strives to understand the characteristics of cooperative work behavior, with the objective of designing adequate technology to support it (Bannon & Schmidt, 1991). Expanding this view to include the objective of developing effective HRM practices within the CSCW environment is essential. As members of an interdisciplinary field that addresses the implications of technology in collaborative work settings, the CSCW community is in a unique position to conduct, facilitate, or otherwise promote research and practices that will prepare organizations to make the most of their most valuable resource in tomorrow's CSCW workplace.

# References

Adrianson, L., & Hjelmquist, E. (1991). Group processes in face-to-face and computer-mediated communication. *Behavior & Information Technology, 10,* 281-296.

Archer, N. P. (1990). A comparison of computer conferences with face-to-face meetings for small group business decisions. *Behaviour & Information Technology, 9,* 307-317.

Asch, S. E. (1956). Studies of independence and conformity: I. A minority of one against a unanimous majority. *Psychological Monographs, 70*(9), 1-70.

Augustine, M. A., & Coovert, M. D. (1991). Simulation and information order as influences in the development of mental models. *Association for Computing Machinery [ACM] SIGCHI [Special Interest Group on Computer-Human Interaction] Bulletin, 23,* 33-35.

Bannon, L. J., & Schmidt, K. (1991). CSCW: Four characters in search of a context. In J. M. Bowers & S. D. Benford (Eds.), *Studies in computer supported cooperative work: Theory, practice and design* (pp. 3-16). North-Holland: Elsevier Science Publishers B.V.

Bass, B. M. (1985). *Leadership and performance beyond expectations.* New York: Free Press.

Bates, J. J. (1994). The role of emotion in believable agents. *Communications of the ACM, 37*(7), 122-125.

Baudel, T., & Beaudouin-Lafon, M. (1993). CHARADE: Remote control of objects using free-hand gestures. *Communications of the ACM, 36,* 28-35.

Bayarri, S., Fernandez, M., & Perez, M. (1996). Virtual reality for driving simulation. *Communications of the ACM, 39*(5), 72-76.

Berwald, M., & Hakel, M. (1999, July). Dateline 2020: A look back at I-O at the turn of the millennium. *The Industrial-Organizational Psychologist, 37*(1), 25-28.

Bird, S. D. (1997). Conceptualizing a shared language subsystem for distributed decision support systems. *Decision Support Systems, 19*(4), 227-235.

Bobick, A. F., Intille, S. S., Davis, J. W., Baird, F., Pinhanez, C. S., Campbell, L. W., Ivanov, Y. A., Schutte, A., & Wilson, A. (2000). The KidsRoom. *Communications of the ACM, 43*(3), 60-61.

Bocionek, S. R. (1995). Agent systems that negotiate and learn. *International Journal of Human-Computer Studies, 42*(3), 265-288.

Bowers, J. M., & Benford, S. D. (1991). *Studies in computer supported cooperative work: Theory, practice and design.* North-Holland: Elsevier Science Publishers B.V.

Bridges, W. (1994, September 19). The end of the job. *Fortune, 130*(6), 62-64, 68, 72, 74.

Buchanan, B. G., & Shortliffe, E. H. (1984). *Rule-based expert systems: The MYCIN experiments of the Stanford heuristic programming project.* Reading, MA: Addison-Wesley.

Cannon-Bowers, J. A., & Salas, E. (1998). Team performance and training in complex environments: Recent findings from applied research. *Current Directions in Psychological Science, 7*(3), 83-87.

Cascio, W. F. (1989). *Managing human resources: Productivity, quality of work life, profits* (2nd ed.). New York: McGraw-Hill.

Cascio, W. F. (1995). Whither industrial and organizational psychology in a changing world of work? *The American Psychologist, 50*(11), 928-939.

Chen, H. C., Houston, A., Nunamaker, J., & Yen, J. (1996). Toward intelligent meeting agents. *Computer, 29*(8), 62-69.

Coen, M. H. (1998). A prototype intelligent environment. In N. A. Streitz, S. Konomi, & H. Burkhardt (Eds.), *Cooperative buildings: Integrating information, organization, and architecture* (pp. 41-52). New York: Springer-Verlag.

Connors, M. M., Harrison, A. A., & Summit, J. (1994). Crew systems: Integrating human and technical subsystems for the exploration of space. *Behavioral Science, 39*(3), 183-212.

Coovert, M. D. (1987). The use of mental models to enhance human-computer interaction. *Association for Computing Machinery SIGCHI Bulletin, 18,* 79-81.

Coovert, M. D. (1988). Analysis and assessment of MIS training needs for naive corporate users: A case study. *Association for Computing Machinery SIGCHI Bulletin, 19,* 56-61.

Coovert, M. D. (1990). Development and evaluation of five user models of human-computer interaction. In U. Gattiker (Ed.), *End-user training* (pp. 105-139). Berlin: Walter de Gryter.

Coovert, M. D. (1995). Technological changes in office jobs: What we know and what to expect. In A. Howard (Ed.), *The changing nature of work* (pp. 175-208). San Francisco: Jossey-Bass.

Coovert, M. D., Craiger, J. P., & Cannon-Bowers, J. A. (1995). Innovations in modeling and simulating team performance: Implications for decision making. In R. A. Guzzo & E. Salas (Eds.), *Team effectiveness and decision making in organizations* (pp. 149-203). San Francisco: Jossey-Bass.

Coovert, M. D., & Foster, L. L. (in press). Technology and health risks at work. In J. C. Quick & L. E. Tetrick (Eds.), *Handbook of occupational health psychology.* Washington, DC: American Psychological Association.

Coovert, M. D., & Goldstein, M. (1980). Locus of control as a predictor of users' attitude toward computers. *Psychological Reports, 47,* 1167-1173.

Coovert, M. D., Salas, E., & Ramakrishna, K. (1992). The role of individual and system characteristics in computerized training systems. *Computers in Human Behavior, 8,* 335-352.

Coury, B. G., & Semmel, R. D. (1996). Supervisory control and the design of intelligent user interfaces. In R. Parasuraman & M. Mouloua (Eds.), *Automation and human performance* (pp. 221-242). Mahwah, NJ: Lawrence Erlbaum.

Covi, L. M., Olson, J. S., & Rocco, E. (1998). A room of your own: What do we learn about support of teamwork from assessing teams in dedicated project rooms? In N. A. Streitz, S. Konomi, & H. Burkhardt (Eds.), *Cooperative buildings: Integrating information, organization, and architecture* (pp. 53-65). New York: Springer-Verlag.

Craiger, J. P. (1997, January). Technology, organizations, and work in the 20th century. *The Industrial-Organizational Psychologist, 34*(3), 89-96.

Crowley, J. L., Coutaz, J., & Berard, F. (2000). Things that see. *Communications of the ACM, 43*(3), 54-64.

Dubrovsky, V. J., Kiesler, S., & Sethna, B. N. (1991). The equalization phenomenon: Status effects in computer-mediated and face-to-face decision-making groups. *Human Computer Interaction, 6,* 119-146.

Ellis, C. A., Gibbs, S. J., & Rein, G. L. (1991). Groupware—some issues and experiences. *Communications of the ACM, 34*(1), 35-58.

Elrod, S., Hall, G., Costanza, R., Dixon, M., & Des Rivieres, J. (1993). Responsive office environments. *Communications of the ACM, 36,* 84-85.

Etzioni, O., & Weld, D. S. (1995). Intelligent agents on the internet: Fact, fiction, and forecast. *IEEE Expert-Intelligent Systems & Their Applications, 10*(4), 44-49.

Feiner, S., MacIntyre, B., & Seligmann, D. (1993). Knowledge-based augmented reality. *Communications of the ACM, 36,* 52-62.

Fitzmaurice, G. W. (1993). Situated information spaces and spatially aware palmtop computers. *Communications of the ACM, 36,* 39-49.

Fitzpatrick, G., Kaplan, S., & Parsowth, S. (1998). Experience in building a cooperative distributed organization: Lessons for cooperative buildings. In N. A. Streitz, S. Konomi, & H. Burkhardt (Eds.), *Cooperative buildings: Integrating information, organization, and architecture* (pp. 66-79). New York: Springer-Verlag.

Foster, L. L., & Coovert, M. D. (1997). The influences of communication media and decision-making technique on team decision outcomes: A critical assessment of the stepladder approach. *Proceedings of the CHI 97 Conference on Human Factors in Computing Systems,* 240-241.

Foster, L. L., & Coovert, M. D. (2000a, April). *E-mail @ work: The effects of computer-mediated communication on team collaboration.* Paper presented at the 15th annual meeting of the Society for Industrial and Organizational Psychology, New Orleans, Louisiana.

Foster, L. L., & Coovert, M. D. (2000b). "Intelligent" team decision making. *Proceedings of the CHI 2000 Conference on Human Factors in Computing Systems,* 153-154.

Gale, S. (1994). Desktop video conferencing: Technical advances and evaluation issues. In S. A. R. Scrivener (Ed.), *Computer-supported cooperative work* (pp. 81-104). Brookfield, VT: Ashgate.

Gallupe, R. B., Bastianutti, L. M., & Cooper, W. H. (1991). Unblocking brainstorms. *Journal of Applied Psychology, 76,* 137-142.

Gallupe, R. B., Cooper, W. H., Grisé, M. L., & Bastianutti, L. M. (1994). Blocking electronic brainstorms. *Journal of Applied Psychology, 79,* 77-86.

Gallupe, R. B., Dennis, A. R., Cooper, W. H., Valacich, J. S., Nunamaker, J. J., & Bastianutti, L. (1992). Electronic brainstorming and group size. *Academy of Management Journal, 35,* 350-369.

Gomes, L., & Bransten, L. (1997, November 17). Computers: Little computers, big new marketing battle. *The Wall Street Journal,* p. B1.

Greenberg, S., & Neuwirth, C. (1998). From the papers co-chairs. *Proceedings of the ACM 98 Conference on Computer Supported Cooperative Work,* v.

Greif, I. (1994). Desktop agents in group-enabled products. *Communications of the ACM, 7*(7), 100-105.

Gwynne, S. C. (1992, September 28). The long haul. *Time,* 34-38.

Hackman, J. R., & Oldham, G. R. (1976). Motivation through the design of work: Test of a theory. *Organizational Behavior and Human Performance, 16,* 250-279.

Han, J., & Smith, B. (1996). CU-SeeMe VR immersive desktop teleconferencing. *Proceedings of the fourth ACM international multimedia conference on ACM Multimedia, 96,* 199.

Hayesroth, F., & Jacobstein, N. (1994). The state of knowledge-based systems. *Communications of the ACM, 37*(3), 27-39.

Hollingshead, A. B. (1996). The rank-order effect in group decision making. *Organizational Behavior and Human Decision Processes, 68,* 181-193.

Hollingshead, A. B., McGrath, J. E., & O'Connor, K. M. (1993). Group task performance and communication technology: A longitudinal study of computer-mediated versus face-to-face work groups. *Small Group Research, 24,* 307-333.

Hopper, A., Harter, A., & Blackie, T. (1993). The active badge system. In S. Ashlund, K. Mullet, A. Henderson, E. Hollnagel, & T. White (Eds.), *Human factors in computing systems: INTERCHI '93 conference proceedings* (pp. 194-197). New York: The Association for Computing Machinery.

Howard, A. (1995). A framework for work change. In A. Howard (Ed.), *The changing nature of work* (pp. 3-44). San Francisco: Jossey-Bass.

Hunt, R., Vanecko, A., & Poltrock, S. (1998). Future@Work: An experimental exhibit investigating integrated workplace design. In N. A. Streitz, S. Konomi, & H. Burkhardt (Eds.), *Cooperative buildings: Integrating information, organization, and architecture* (pp. 177-190). New York: Springer-Verlag.

Hutchins, E. (1995). *Cognition in the wild.* Cambridge, MA: MIT.

Ilgen, D. R. (1999). Teams embedded in organizations: Some implications. *American Psychologist, 54*(2), 129-139.

Ishii, H., & Ullmer, B. (1997). Tangible bits: Towards seamless interfaces between people, bits and atoms. *CHI 97 Conference proceedings on human factors in computing systems* (pp. 234-241). New York: Association for Computing Machinery.

Jackson, R. L., Taylor, W., & Winn, W. (1999). Peer collaboration and virtual environments: A preliminary investigation of multi-participant virtual reality applied to science application. *Proceedings of the 1999 ACM symposium on applied computing 1999,* 121-125.

Janis, I. L. (1982). *Groupthink: Psychological studies of policy decisions and fiascoes.* Boston: Houghton Mifflin.

Johansen, R. (1988). *Groupware: Computer support for business teams.* New York: Free Press.

Johnson, D. W., & Johnson, F. P. (1994). *Joining together: Group theory and group skills* (5th ed.). Boston: Allyn and Bacon.

Jones, B. (1995). *Sleepers, wake: Technology and the future of work* (4th ed.). Melbourne: Oxford University.

Keates, N. (1997, December 3). As airfares soar, more companies cancel trips. *The Wall Street Journal,* p. B1.

Kiechel, W., III, & Sacha, B. (1993, May 17). How we will work in the year 2000. *Fortune, 127*(10), 38-52.

Kiesler, S., Siegel, J., & McGuire, T. W. (1984). Social psychological aspects of computer-mediated communication. *American Psychologist, 39,* 1123-1134.

Kiesler, S., & Sproull, L. (1992). Group decision making and communication technology. *Organizational Behavior and Human Decision Processes, 52,* 96-123.

Kirsh, D. (1998). Adaptive rooms, virtual collaboration and cognitive workflow. In N. A. Streitz, S. Konomi, & H. Burkhardt (Eds.), *Cooperative buildings: Integrating information, organization, and architecture* (pp. 94-106). New York: Springer-Verlag.

LaLomia, M. J., & Coovert, M. D. (1987). A comparison of tabular and graphical displays in four problem solving domains. *Association for Computing Machinery SIGCHI Bulletin, 19,* 49-54.

LaLomia, M. J., & Coovert, M. D. (1988). Problem solving performance and display preference for information displays depicting numerical functions. *Association for Computing Machinery SIGCHI Bulletin, 20,* 47-51.

LaLomia, M. J., & Coovert, M. D. (1992). Problem solving performance as a function of problem type, number progression, and memory load. *Behaviour and Information Technology, 11,* 268-280.

Lee, J., Su, J., Ren, S., Ishii, H., Hsiao, J., & Hongladaromp, R. (1999). *HandSCAPE. SIGGRPHA'99 special interest group on computer graphics: Emerging technologies, 166.* New York: The Association for Computing Machinery.

Lenat, D. B. (1995). CYC: A large-scale investment in knowledge infrastructure. *Communications of the ACM, 38*(11), 33-38.

Lenat, D. B., & Guha, R. V. (1994). *Ideas for applying CYC.* Retrieved May 21, 2000 from the World Wide Web: www.cyc.com/tech-reports/act-cyc-407-91/act-cyc-407-91.html.

Levine, E. L. (1983). *Everything you always wanted to know about job analysis.* Tampa, FL: Mariner.

Lieberman, H. (1997). Autonomous interface agents. Proceedings of the *CHI 97 Conference on Human Factors in Computing Systems, 67-74.*

Mackay, W., Velay, G., Carter, K., Ma, C., & Pagani, D. (1993). Augmenting reality: Adding computational dimensions to paper. *Communications of the ACM, 36,* 96-97.

Maes, P. (1994). Agents that reduce work and information overload. *Communications of the ACM, 37*(7), 31-40.

Magedanz, T. (1995). On the impacts of intelligent agent concepts on future telecommunication environments. In A. Clarke, M. Campolargo, & N. Karatzas (Eds.), *Bringing Telecommunication Services to the People—IS&N'95* (pp. 396-414). New York: Springer.

Maier, N. R. F. (1967). Assets and liabilities in group problem solving: The need for an integrative function. *Psychological Review, 74,* 239-249.

Mann, S. (1996). 'Smart clothing': Wearable multimedia and 'personal imaging' to restore the balance between people and their intelligent environments. *Proceedings of the ACM 96 Multimedia,* 18-22.

Mann, S. (1998). Wearable computing as a means for personal empowerment. *Proceedings of The First International Conference on Wearable Computing, ICWC-98, 83,* 2123-2151.

Mathieu, J. E., & Zajac, D. M. (1990). A review and meta-analysis of the antecedents, correlates, and consequences of organizational commitment. *Psychological Bulletin, 108,* 171-194.

McGuire, T. W., Kiesler, S., & Siegel, J. (1987). Group and computer-mediated discussion effects in risk decision making. *Journal of Personality and Social Psychology, 52,* 917-930.

McLeod, P. L. (1992). An assessment of the experimental literature on electronic support of group work: Results of a meta-analysis. *Human-Computer Interaction, 7,* 257-280.

McLeod, P. L., Baron, R. S., Marti, M. W., & Yoon, K. (1997). The eyes have it: Minority influence in face-to-face and computer-mediated group discussion. *Journal of Applied Psychology, 82,* 706-718.

Meyer, J. P., Allen, N. J., & Smith, C. A. (1993). Commitment to organizations and occupations: Extension and test of a three-component conceptualization. *Journal of Applied Psychology, 78,* 538-551.

Milewski, A. E., & Lewis, S. H. (1997). Delegating to software agents. *International Journal of Human-Computer Studies, 46*(4), 485-500.

Mitchell, T., Caruana, R., Freitag, D., McDermott, J., & Zabowski, D. (1994). Experience with a learning personal assistant. *Communications of the ACM, 37*(7), 81-91.

Moltke, I., & Andersen, H. H. K. (1998). Cooperative buildings—The case of office VISION. In N. A. Streitz, S. Konomi, & H. Burkhardt (Eds.), *Cooperative buildings: Integrating information, organization, and architecture* (pp. 163-176). New York: Springer-Verlag.

Montazemi, A. R., & Gupta, K. M. (1997). On the effectiveness of cognitive feedback from an interface agent. *Omega-International Journal of Management Science, 25*(6), 643-658.

Newell, A., & Simon, H. A. (1961). GPS, a program that simulates human thought. In H. Billing (Ed.), *Lernede Automaten* (pp. 109-124). Munich, Germany: R. Oldenbourg.

Olaniran, B. A. (1996). A model of group satisfaction in computer-mediated communication and face-to-face meetings. *Behaviour & Information Technology, 15,* 24-36.

Oviatt, S., & Cohen, P. (2000). Multimodal interfaces that process what comes naturally. *Communications of the ACM, 43*(3), 45-53.

Pearson, C. A. L., & Chong, J. (1997). Contributions of job content and social information on organizational commitment and job satisfaction: An exploration in a Malaysian nursing context. *Journal of Occupational and Organizational Psychology, 70,* 357-374.

Pentland, A. (2000). Perceptual intelligence. *Communications of the ACM, 43*(3), 35-44.

Peters, T. J., & Waterman, R. H., Jr. (1982). *In search of excellence: Lessons from America's best-run companies.* New York: Harper & Row.

Picard, R. W. (2000). Affective perception. *Communications of the ACM, 43*(3), 50-51.

Raghavan, A. (1993, July 9). Amex specialists test hand-held computers. *The Wall Street Journal,* p. B1.

Rhodes, B. J. (1997). The wearable Remembrance Agent: a system for augmented memory. *Personal Technologies Journal Special Issue on Wearable Computing, Personal Technologies, 1,* 218-224.

Rich, B. R. (1994). *Skunk works: A personal memoir of my years at Lockheed.* Boston: Little, Brown.

Riecken, D. (1994). M: An architecture of integrated agents. *Communications of the ACM, 37*(7), 107-116.

Riggio, R. E. (1990). *Introduction to industrial/organizational psychology.* Glenview, IL: Scott, Foresman.

Rodger, J. A., & Pendharkar, P. C. (2000). Using telemedicine in the department of defense. *Communications of the ACM, 43*(3), 19-20.

Roesler, M., & Hawkins, D. T. (1994). Intelligent agents: Software servants for an electronic information world (and more). *Online, 18*(4), 18-32.

Rue, L. W., & Byars, L. L. (1980). *Management: Theory and application* (2nd ed.). Homewood, IL: Richard D. Irwin.

Sarma, V. V. S. (1996). Intelligent agents. *Journal of the Institution of Electronics and Telecommunication Engineers, 42*(3), 105-109.

Scrivener, S. A. R. (1994). *Computer-supported cooperative work.* Brookfield, VT: Ashgate.

Scrivener, S. A. R., & Clark, S. (1994). Introducing computer-supported cooperative work. In S. A. R. Scrivener (Ed.), *Computer-supported cooperative work* (pp. 19-38). Brookfield, VT: Ashgate.

Selker, T. (1994). COACH: A teaching agent that learns. *Communications of the ACM, 37*(7), 92-99.

Sen, S., Haynes, T., & Arora, N. (1997). Satisfying user preferences while negotiating meetings. *International Journal of Human-Computer Studies, 47*(3), 407-427.

Siegel, J., Dubrovsky, V., Kiesler, S., & McGuire, T. W. (1986). Group processes in computer-mediated communication. *Organizational Behavior and Human Decision Processes, 37,* 157-187.

Smilowitz, M., Compton, D. C., & Flint, L. (1988). The effects of computer mediated communication on an individual's judgment: A study based on the methods of Asch's social influence experiment. *Computers in Human Behavior, 4,* 311-321.

Spector, P. E. (2000). *Industrial and organizational psychology: Research and practice* (2nd ed.). New York: John Wiley & Sons.

Spurr, K., Layzell, P., Jennison, L., & Richards, N. (1994). *Computer support for co-operative work.* West Sussex, England: John Wiley & Sons.

Straus, S. G. (1996). Getting a clue: The effects of communication media and information distribution on participation and performance in computer-mediated and face-to-face groups. *Small Group Research, 27,* 115-142.

Straus, S. G., & McGrath, J. E. (1994). Does the medium matter? The interaction of task type and technology on group performance and member reactions. *Journal of Applied Psychology, 79,* 87-97.

Streitz, N. A., Konomi, S., & Burkhardt, H. (Eds.). (1998). *Cooperative buildings: Integrating information, organization, and architecture.* Berlin: Springer.

Swezey, R.W., & Salas, E. (Eds.). (1992). *Teams: Their training and performance.* Norwood, NJ: Ablex.

Tan, H. Z. (2000). Haptic interfaces. *Communications of the ACM, 43*(3), 40-41.

Tapscott, D., & Caston, A. (1993). *Paradigm shift: The new promise of information technology.* New York: McGraw-Hill.

Tilgher, A. (1977). *Work: What it has meant to men through the ages.* New York: Harcourt Brace.

Turk, M., & Robertson, G. (2000). Perceptual user interfaces. *Communications of the ACM, 43*(3), 33-34.

Ullmer, B., Glas, D., & Ishii, H. (1998). MediaBlocks: Physical containers, transports, and controls for online media. *Proceedings of the 25th annual conference on Computer Graphics,* 379-386.

Valacich, J. S., & Schwenk, C. (1995). Devil's advocacy and dialectical inquiry effects on face-to-face and computer-mediated group decision making. *Organizational Behavior and Human Decision Processes, 63,* 158-173.

Van der Spiegel, J. (1995). New information technologies and changes in work. In A. Howard (Ed.), *The changing nature of work* (pp. 97-111). San Francisco: Jossey-Bass.

Walther, J. B., Anderson, J. F., & Park, D. (1994). Interpersonal effects in computer-mediated interaction: A meta-analysis of social and anti-social communication. *Communication Research, 21,* 460-487.

Weisband, S. P. (1992). Group discussion and first advocacy effects in computer-mediated and face-to-face decision making groups. *Organizational Behavior and Human Decision Processes, 53,* 352-380.

Weiser, M. (1991). The computer for the 21st century. *Scientific American, 265,* 94-104.

Weiser, M. (1993). Some computer science issues in ubiquitous computing. *Communications of the ACM, 36,* 74-84.

Wellner, M. (1993). Interacting with paper on the DigitalDesk. *Communications of the ACM, 36,* 86-96.

Wexelblat, A. (1995). An approach to natural gesture in virtual environments. *ACM Transactions on Computer-Human Interactions, 2*(3), 179-200.

Wilson, P. (1991). *Computer supported cooperative work.* Oxford, England: Intellect.

Wilson, P. (1994). Introducing CSCW: What it is and why we need it. In S. A. R. Scrivener (Ed.), *Computer-supported cooperative work* (pp. 1-18). Brookfield, VT: Ashgate.

Yan, Y., & Ramaswamy, S. (1998). Interactive, agent based, modeling and simulation of virtual manufacturing assemblies. *Proceedings of the 36th annual conference on Southeast regional conference,* 78-87.

Yarin, P., & Ishii, H. (1999). *TouchCounters: designing interactive electronic labels for physical containers. Proceedings of the CHI 99 Conference on Human Factors in Computing Systems,* 362-369.

Zajtchuk, R., & Satava, R. M. (1997). Medical applications of virtual reality. *Communications of the ACM, 40*(9), 63-64.

Ziegler, B. (1994, October 12). Video conference calls change business. *The Wall Street Journal,* p. B1.

# *Index*

# About the Authors

**Michael D. Coovert** is Professor and Associate Chair in the Department of Psychology at the University of South Florida where he is also the founding director of The Institute for Human Performance, Decision Making, and Cybernetics. Dr. Coovert received an undergraduate degree in computer science and psychology from Chaminade University, a master's in psychology from Illinois State University, and a PhD in psychology (with a doctoral minor in computer science) from The Ohio State University. He consults and publishes widely on research in the areas of performance measurement, teams, quantitative methods, human computer interaction, and computer supported cooperative work (CSCW).

**Lori Foster Thompson** joined the faculty of East Carolina University as an Assistant Professor of Psychology in the fall of 1999. She received a BA in Psychology from Augusta State University in 1994, and she obtained both MA and PhD degrees in Industrial/Organizational Psychology from the University of South Florida in 1997 and 1999 respectively. She completed a minor in Instructional Technology as part of her graduate studies. Dr. Thompson's research, which appears regularly at national and international conferences, has been published in professional journals such as *Human Performance*. Her research interests focus on CSCW, individual and team performance measurement, and criterion development. She is an active member of The Society for

Industrial and Organizational Psychology (SIOP), and she currently coauthors a column for SIOP's quarterly publication of The Industrial-Organizational Psychologist (TIP)

Printed in the United States
By Bookmasters